W9-CPY-384

WILDLIFE
and PLANTS
of the world

An updated and expanded edition of *Wildlife of the World*

now including plants, microorganisms, and biomes

Volume 9

Marshall Cavendish
New York • London • Toronto • Sydney

Marshall Cavendish Corporation
99 White Plains Road
Tarrytown, New York 10591-9001

Created by **Brown Partworks Ltd**

Library of Congress Cataloging-in-Publication Data

Wildlife and plants of the world.
    p.   cm.
    Includes bibliographical references and index.
    Summary: Alphabetically-arranged illustrated articles introduce over 350 animals, plants, and habitats and efforts to protect them.
    ISBN 0-7614-7099-9 (set : lib. bdg. : alk. paper)
    1. Animals—Juvenile literature. 2. Plants—Juvenile literature.
[1. Animals. 2. Plants.] I. Marshall Cavendish Corporation.
QL49.W539   1998
578—DC21   97-32139
                                    CIP
                                      AC

ISBN 0-7614-7099-9 (set)
ISBN 0-7614-7108-1 (vol.9)

Printed in Malaysia
Bound in the United States

Brown Packaging

Editorial consultants:
- Joshua Ginsberg, Ph.D.
- Jefferey Kaufmann, Ph.D.
- Paul Sieswerda, Ph.D.
  (Wildlife Conservation Society)
- Special thanks to the Dept. of Botany, The Natural History Museum, U.K.

Editors:	Deborah Evans
	Leon Gray
Assistant editor:	Amanda Harman
Art editors:	Joan Curtis
	Alison Gardner
	Sandra Horth
Picture researchers:	Amanda Baker
	Brenda Clynch
Illustrations:	Bill Botten
	John Francis

Marshall Cavendish Corporation

Editorial director:	Paul Bernabeo
Project editor:	Debra M. Jacobs
Editorial consultant:	Elizabeth Kaplan

PICTURE CREDITS
The publishers would like to thank Natural History Photographic Agency, Ardingly, Sussex, U.K., for supplying the following pictures:
A.N.T. (Bruce Thomson) 524, 530, 540, 560, 561; Henry Ausloos 548; Anthony Bannister 562; G. I. Bernard 533, 535, 567; Joe B. Blossom 519, 544; Laurie Campbell 520, 521, 532, 539; James H. Carmichael Jr. 553; Stephen Dalton 568 (left), 568 (right), 566; Nigel J. Dennis 528, 563; Douglas Dickins 534; K. Ghani 569; Brian Hawkes 522, 552, 564; Daniel Heuclin 543; E. A. Janes 559; Peter Johnson 518; B. Jones & M. Shimlock 531; Stephen Krasemann 526, 527, 538, 542, 565, 570, 571; Gerard Lacz 529, 550; Michael Leach 573; Trevor McDonald 537; Haroldo Palo 549; William S. Paton 574; Jany Sauvenet 525, 545, 558; John Shaw 554, 555, 572, 575; Eric Soder 523.

Additional pictures supplied by:
Heather Angel 546, 547; Oxford Scientific Films 536, 551; Planet Earth Pictures 556.

Front cover
Main image: Female lion playing with cubs, photographed by Gerard Lacz.
Additional image: Californian or Gold poppy, photographed by John Shaw.

Status

In the Key Facts on the species described in this publication, you will find details of the appearance, name (both Latin and common name wherever possible), breeding habits, and so on. The status of an organism indicates how common it is. The status of each organism is based on reference works prepared by two organizations: *1996 IUCN Red List of Threatened Animals* published by the International Union for Conservation of Nature and Natural Resources (IUCN) and *Endangered and Threatened Wildlife and Plants* published in 1997 by the United States Government Printing Office (USGPO)

Extinct:	No sighting in the last 40 years
Endangered:	In danger of becoming extinct
Threatened:	A species that will become endangered if its present condition in the wild continues to deteriorate
Rare:	Not threatened, but not frequently found in the wild
In captivity:	A species that is extinct in the wild but has been kept successfully in captivity
Feral:	Animals that have been domesticated and have escaped into the wild
Common:	Frequently found within its range, which may be limited
Widespread:	Commonly found in many parts of the world

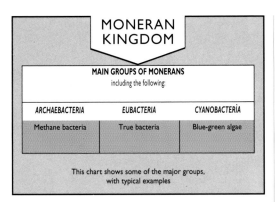

MONERAN KINGDOM

MAIN GROUPS OF MONERANS		
including the following:		
ARCHAEBACTERIA	EUBACTERIA	CYANOBACTERÌA
Methane bacteria	True bacteria	Blue-green algae

This chart shows some of the major groups, with typical examples

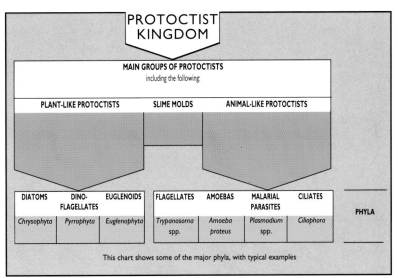

PROTOCTIST KINGDOM

MAIN GROUPS OF PROTOCTISTS							
including the following:							
PLANT-LIKE PROTOCTISTS			SLIME MOLDS	ANIMAL-LIKE PROTOCTISTS			
DIATOMS	DINO-FLAGELLATES	EUGLENOIDS		FLAGELLATES	AMOEBAS	MALARIAL PARASITES	CILIATES
Chrysophyta	Pyrrophyta	Euglenophyta		Trypanosoma spp.	Amoeba proteus	Plasmodium spp.	Ciliophora

PHYLA

This chart shows some of the major phyla, with typical examples

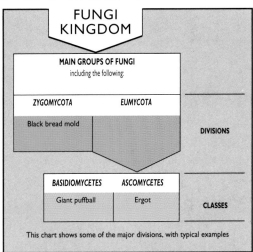

FUNGI KINGDOM

MAIN GROUPS OF FUNGI	
including the following:	
ZYGOMYCOTA	EUMYCOTA
Black bread mold	

DIVISIONS

| BASIDIOMYCETES | ASCOMYCETES |
| Giant puffball | Ergot |

CLASSES

This chart shows some of the major divisions, with typical examples

Moneran, protoctist, and fungi kingdoms

Three groups of living things are not classified in the animal and plant kingdoms. These are the moneran, protoctist, and fungi kingdoms. Monerans are tiny, single-celled organisms that have no distinct nucleus. The nucleus is the control center of the cell. In contrast, protoctists and fungi have visibly distinct nuclei and tiny organs (called organelles). However, classification is a topic for much debate, and many scientists disagree on the classification of organisms in these three kingdoms.

The moneran kingdom contains all the microscopic, single-celled organisms that do not have distinct nuclei. The three main groups of monerans are: true bacteria, blue-green algae, and methane bacteria. The largest group of monerans is the true bacteria (*Eubacteria*).

For over a billion years, bacteria were the only living things on the earth. Then about 1.5 billion years ago, new organisms, called protoctists (formerly known as protists), evolved from the methane bacteria. All protoctists are single-celled organisms, but their cell structure is more complex than monerans. For example, protoctists have nuclei.

Scientists tend to classify an organism as a protoctist when they cannot place the organism in the animal, plant, or fungi kingdoms. Protoctists are grouped into phyla that have animal-, plant-, or fungus-like features. Single-celled algae, such as diatoms and euglenoids, behave like plants. Amoebas can move about and are more like animals. Slime molds form a subkingdom that have characteristics similar to the fungi kingdom.

Fungi make up the last kingdom of living things. Mushrooms, toadstools, and molds are all fungi. Fungi differ from animals and plants in that they depend on other organisms for their food. Like plants, fungi form groups called divisions. There are two divisions in the fungi kingdom.

See Volume 17 for more information on monerans, protoctists, and fungi.

COLOR GUIDE

MONERANS, PROTOCTISTS, & FUNGI

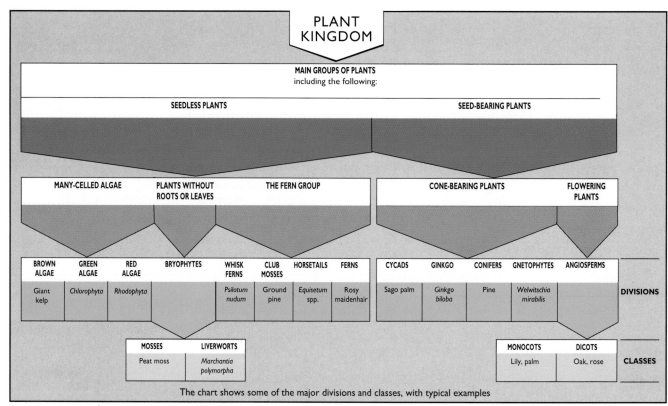

PLANT KINGDOM

The chart shows some of the major divisions and classes, with typical examples

The plant kingdom

Every plant, from the tiniest shrub to the tallest tree, belongs to the plant kingdom. There are about 500,000 different kinds (species) of plant that have been identified.

The plant kingdom (shown above) can be divided into 13 divisions. A plant division is similar to a phylum in animal classification. Each division represents a number of classes of plants that all have certain features in common.

The simplest plants are algae, all of which live in water. This set of books classifies three divisions of multicellular (or many-celled) algae in the plant kingdom. Some scientists, though, prefer to classify multicellular algae as protoctists.

Two classes, mosses and liverworts, make up the bryophyte division. These plants lack the roots, stems, and leaves that are found in other plant divisions.

The fern group comprises four divisions of the plant kingdom: whisk ferns, club mosses, horsetails, and ferns. All members of the fern group have two stages in their life cycle. During one of these stages tiny reproductive structures, called spores, are released. These spores will eventually grow into a new plant.

More complex plants reproduce with seeds. Four divisions of plants reproduce with "naked" seeds in cones. Cycads, conifers, ginkgoes, and gnetophytes are all cone-bearing plants.

Two classes, monocots and dicots, make up the largest division of plants, the angiosperms, or flowering plants. Unlike cone-bearing plants, angiosperms reproduce with enclosed seeds such as berries, nuts, and fruits.

See Volume 17 for more information on the different divisions of plants.

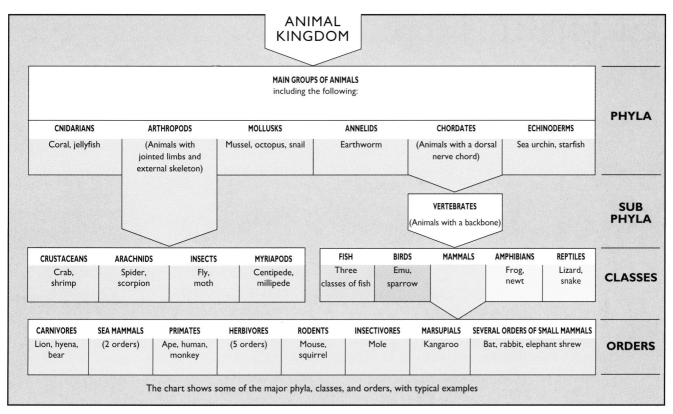

ANIMAL KINGDOM

MAIN GROUPS OF ANIMALS
including the following:

PHYLA

CNIDARIANS	ARTHROPODS	MOLLUSKS	ANNELIDS	CHORDATES	ECHINODERMS
Coral, jellyfish	(Animals with jointed limbs and external skeleton)	Mussel, octopus, snail	Earthworm	(Animals with a dorsal nerve chord)	Sea urchin, starfish

SUB PHYLA

VERTEBRATES
(Animals with a backbone)

CLASSES

CRUSTACEANS	ARACHNIDS	INSECTS	MYRIAPODS	FISH	BIRDS	MAMMALS	AMPHIBIANS	REPTILES
Crab, shrimp	Spider, scorpion	Fly, moth	Centipede, millipede	Three classes of fish	Emu, sparrow		Frog, newt	Lizard, snake

ORDERS

CARNIVORES	SEA MAMMALS	PRIMATES	HERBIVORES	RODENTS	INSECTIVORES	MARSUPIALS	SEVERAL ORDERS OF SMALL MAMMALS
Lion, hyena, bear	(2 orders)	Ape, human, monkey	(5 orders)	Mouse, squirrel	Mole	Kangaroo	Bat, rabbit, elephant shrew

The chart shows some of the major phyla, classes, and orders, with typical examples

The animal kingdom

In the eighteenth century, a botanist from Sweden named Carl von Linné (usually known by his Latin name, *Carolus Linneaus*) outlined a system of classifying plants and animals. This became the basis for classification all over the world. Scientists use Latin names so that all plants, animals, and other living things can be identified accurately, even though they have different common names in different places. Linneaus divided living organisms into two kingdoms: plants and animals. Today most scientists divide living things into five kingdoms: animals, plants, monerans, protoctists, and fungi. The animal kingdom (*above*) is divided into many phyla. Most of the phyla of the animal kingdom contain strange creatures – microscopic organisms, sponges, corals, slugs, and insects – without the backbone and central nervous system that we associate with more familiar animals.

Each phylum is divided into classes. For example, vertebrates (animals with a backbone) are a subdivision of a phylum and are divided up into seven classes: mammals, birds, reptiles, amphibians, and three classes of fish (represented by eels, sharks, and trout).

Each of these classes is broken down further into different orders. The mammal class, for instance, includes the orders carnivores (meat eaters), insectivores (insect eaters), primates (monkeys, apes), and marsupials (kangaroos, koalas), among others.

In this set of books, we give Latin names for different groups (genera) and kinds (species) of animals. See Volume 17 for more information on the different phyla of animals.

COLOR GUIDE

INVERTEBRATES

FISH

AMPHIBIANS & REPTILES

BIRDS

MAMMALS

PLANTS

BIOMES & HABITATS

MONERANS, PROTOCTISTS, & FUNGI

Leopard

The leopard is beautiful but deadly. Prized for its golden fur with dark spots, this big cat is also one of the animal world's best lone hunters. It is one of the strongest of the large carnivores (meat eaters), and one of the fastest, too.

Everything about the leopard makes it an efficient fighting machine. It locates its prey easily because it has sharp eyesight, a fine sense of smell, and very good hearing. Its muscular body and legs give it good sprinting and jumping ability, so it can leap onto its prey after a short chase or in an ambush. Then, the leopard uses its powerful shoulders, strong jaws, and sharp teeth to kill small victims at once by breaking their necks. It suffocates larger animals by sinking its teeth into their throats until they choke.

Leopards depend very heavily on trees for their success as hunters. Their short, powerful legs and strong claws enable them to leap up into branches and to maintain balance; their spotted markings make them difficult to see in the patches of light and shadow created by the leaves. Other species of carnivore with which the leopard competes for its prey – from hunting dogs to lions or cheetahs – cannot use trees in the same way.

Storing food in trees

Leopards also use trees as a larder. They will haul their kill into a tree, laying it across a branch, to keep it safe from scavengers such as hyenas, jackals, or lions so they can come back and make a second meal. Once again, the power of the leopard is important here. A leopard can pick up a victim in its jaws and use the strength of its muscular legs to drag an animal into the branches – and sometimes these animals may weigh as much as the leopard itself!

Finally, leopards use trees for protection from their greatest natural enemy, lions.

KEY FACTS

- **Name**
  Leopard
  (*Panthera pardus*)

- **Range**
  Africa, Asia, Middle East, Sri Lanka, Java

- **Habitat**
  Semideserts, grasslands, forests, jungles, mountains

- **Appearance**
  Long body, measuring 6 ft (1.8 m) plus a tail of 4 ft (1.2 m); short legs; a small head and ears; golden-brown fur with dark, boxy spots

- **Food**
  Ground birds, and small mammals

- **Breeding**
  Up to 6 cubs (usually 2 or 3); the cubs are weaned at 3 months and leave the mother at about 2 years

- **Status**
  Endangered

◄ *This leopard is alert and on the lookout for danger. It has a solid, muscular body, short legs, and powerful shoulders.*

Lions may attack any leopards that enter their hunting grounds, but if leopards can escape into trees, then they are safe because the lions cannot follow them into the branches. Where there are few trees – such as on the Serengeti Plains of East Africa – there are few leopards because the lions drive them out.

Learning to hunt

From an early age, leopards learn to be hunters. There are normally two or three cubs in a litter, and from about three months old they play at hunting, starting by stalking small animals like mice and rats and moving onto larger victims such as young antelopes or large birds when they get older. By the time they leave their mother to fend for themselves – at about two years old – they have developed all the skills they will need.

Leopards are in danger of extinction in many parts of their range, mainly due to human interference. Leopards have a reputation for attacking people, and although such attacks are, in fact, very

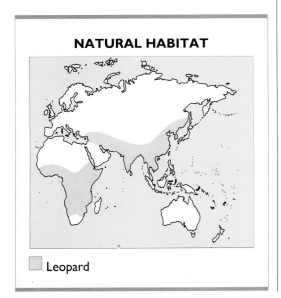

NATURAL HABITAT

☐ Leopard

rare, villagers shoot them on sight. The main reason humans have hunted the leopard, however, is for its beautiful spotted fur. The markings that make the animal so difficult to see in the trees have put a price on its head: the hunter has become the hunted. And although there is a ban on trading in leopard skins, there are still poachers who illegally trap these rare and magnificent animals.

Related to the leopard?

Although often classified as a big cat like the leopard, the Clouded leopard (*Neofelis nebulosa*) is more closely related to small cats such as the lynx (*Felis lynx*) or bobcat (*Felis rufus*). It is found in tropical forests throughout parts of Asia and Indochina, although it is now very rare.

Similarly, the Snow leopard, or ounce, (*Panthera uncia*) is a separate species, although it is more closely related to the true leopard. This species is found in mountainous regions in central Asia, at altitudes of 8900-19,700 ft (2700-6000 m). It is also very rare due to illegal hunting.

▲ *All-black leopards, like the beautiful animal shown above, have often mistakenly been called "Black panthers" and in some cases were thought to be a separate species. However, scientists now know that panthers are, in fact, a black form of true leopards. Interestingly, these animals are more common in Asia, where the animals live in darker, denser forests, than they are in Africa.*

See also **Lion, Mountain**

519

Lichen

Have you ever noticed a crusty patch of color growing on a rock, a tree, or on the side of an old, stone building? If so, you have seen lichens. Before microscopes became widely available, scientists thought lichens were one organism. However, when they looked more closely at lichens they noticed that they were really two completely different organisms – one a light-sensitive organism (usually an alga but less commonly a light-sensitive bacterium), the other a fungus – living together in a close association. The scientific term for this arrangement is "symbiosis."

Give and take

The symbiotic association works like this. The alga or light-sensitive bacterium produces sugars for the fungus to live on by a process called photosynthesis. In return, the fungus shelters and shades its partner. The fungus makes the pigments that give the lichen its color.

Scientists called botanists classify lichens according to the fungi they contain – most species are sac fungi (*Ascomycetes*); there are a few toadstool-like fungi (*Basidiomycetes*); others do not form fruiting bodies (the visible part of the fungi), so they are difficult to classify.

Altogether, the alga and fungus that make up a lichen are extremely important to each other, enabling them to grow in environments as diverse and extreme as the scorching hot desert or the freezing cold tundra.

How do lichens grow?

Lichens, like fungi, have no leaves, roots, or stems. Instead, lichens consist of tiny alga cells mixed up with thread-like fungi.

NATURAL HABITAT

Reindeer lichens (*Cladonia* spp.)

▼ *Lichens such as Cladonia bellidiflora can survive the harsh Arctic climate. They are typically found growing on the surface of rocks and trees.*

▶ *Lichens often hang from tree branches. Lichens that grow on surfaces without soil rely on rain for water and nutrients.*

Lichens grow very slowly, sometimes by as little as 1/25 in (1 mm) each year. They generally live for a very long time: some Arctic lichens are thought to be more than 4000 years old. Lichens may reproduce by vegetative means; that is, portions of existing lichen either break off and fall away or else are carried by browsing animals to begin a new growth elsewhere. Lichens may also reproduce by spores.

Distribution of lichens

There are around 30,000 species of lichen throughout the world. They are found in an enormous variety of habitats, including dry deserts, moist forests, on mountain tops, on soil, and on coastal rocks. Lichens form beard-, crust-, leaf-, or shrub-like growths, richly colored in blues, grays, greens, oranges, and yellows. Beard lichens (*Usnea* spp.) are typically found in damp woods in the northern hemisphere and grow in long, gray-green streamers that hang from tree branches. The cascading streamers can grow up to 3 ft (1 m) long. Other lichens never grow more than a fraction of an inch.

Lichens and their uses

In Arctic regions, cup- and shrub-like reindeer lichens (*Cladonia* spp.) are an important part of the diet of North American caribou and European caribou (reindeer). Lichens make up to 70 percent of these animals' diet. However, the lichens are also harvested by people native to Arctic regions, such as the Lapps from northern Scandinavia in Europe. As a result, reindeer numbers must be controlled to prevent them from eating too much of this valuable resource.

Many lichens are brightly colored and several species are gathered for the pigments that they contain. Orchil is a red or violet dye obtained from lichens of the group (genus) *Roccella*. It is also the source of litmus, which is a substance that changes color from blue to red when placed in acids (such as orange juice) and from red to blue when placed in alkalis (such as milk). Chemists often use litmus to monitor chemical reactions.

KEY FACTS

● **Name**
Cup- or shrub-like reindeer lichen (*Cladonia* spp.)

● **Range**
Wide distribution throughout both the northern and southern hemispheres

● **Habitat**
Found growing on tree bark, on the ground, or on rocks, typically in alpine and mountainous regions

● **Appearance**
Forms small or large clumps of small scales bearing cup-like structures; may also develop miniature shrub-like growths, which form large mats

● **Life cycle**
Portions of the parent lichen break off and fall away or else are carried to form a new lichen elsewhere; may also reproduce by spores

● **Uses**
Food and winter animal feed (called fodder); extracts used for medicine

● **Status**
Widespread

See also **Alga, Bacterium, Caribou, Desert, Fungus, Tundra**

Lily

True lilies are flowering plants (angiosperms) that belong to the group (genus) *Lilium* of the lily family (*Liliaceae*). With 288 subfamilies (genera) and over 4900 different kinds (species), *Liliaceae* is one of the largest families of flowering plants in the world.

Rich variety

True lilies are some of the most beautiful and sought-after of all the flowering plants. They are upright plants with leafy stems, narrow leaves, and scaly bulbs. The

▲ *The pinkish-red flowers of the Turk's cap lily (Lilium superbum) bloom from late July to early September. Each flower of the Turk's cap lily has six petal-like segments, which curve back at the tip (reflex) to form a turban-like shape.*

genus contains between 80 and 100 species that occur naturally in the moderately cold (temperate) regions of the northern hemisphere. Plants of most species are 1-4 ft (0.3-1.2 m) in height. However, certain species may grow to 8 ft (2.5 m). Unlike the fleshy fruits of other flowering plants, the fruit of the lily is a dry capsule.

Lilies are flowering plants. There are two kinds of flowering plants. They are told apart by the number of seed leaves (cotyledons) they have. A cotyledon is a tiny leaf that forms within a seed (from the Greek word *kotyledon,* meaning "cup-shaped"). *Dicotyledonae*, or dicots, have two seed leaves; *Monocotyledonae*, or monocots, have one seed leaf. All true lilies are monocots.

Lily flowers

The flowers of all *Lilium* species have six petal-like segments called tepals. The flowers may stand up like a cup, lie on

NATURAL HABITAT

Original habitat of Turk's cap lily

their side like a funnel, or hang down like a bell or a turban.

In some lilies, such as the Turk's cap lily (*Lilium superbum*), the tepals curve back (reflex). Lily flowers may be solitary or clustered, and they may occur in a wide variety of colors. The inner surface of the flower is often spotted. The flowers of some species have a very pleasant aroma.

Growing lilies

Lilies are usually raised from bulbs. A bulb is a short, flattened or disk-shaped, underground stem, with many fleshy, overlapping leaves filled with stored food. Lilies may also be grown from seed. Different species require different amounts of sunlight, but most prefer a rich, well-drained, loamy soil (consisting of a mixture of clay, sand, and decaying organic material). Most species bloom in July or early August, but some flower in late spring; others bloom in late summer or early in the fall.

Highly prized flowers

The lily is a valuable ornamental plant, and many species are known to have been cultivated in gardens for more than 3000 years. In Asia Minor (present-day Turkey) in the second millennium B.C., the bulb of

the Madonna lily (*Lilium candidum*) was grown for use in medicinal ointments. In Asia and elsewhere, the bulbs have been grown for food.

Since 1950, about 1000 new varieties (called cultivars) of lilies have been bred and registered all over the world using a technique called selective breeding. Selective breeding is the process by which plants are bred for specific characteristics such as color, size, or taste.

Meet the family

Among the popular ornamental plants that belong to the lily family are bluebells (*Hyacinthoides* spp.), snowdrops (*Galanthus* spp.), and tulips (*Tulipa* spp.). Important food plants in this family include asparagus (*Asparagus officinalis*), garlic (*Allium sativum*), and onions (*Allium cepa*).

Many plants that are commonly called lilies are not true lilies. These include the day lilies (*Hemerocallis* spp.), Lily of the field (*Anemone coronaria*), and Lily of the valley (*Convallaria majalis*).

◀ *The red and orange flowers of the Bulb-bearing lily (Lilium bulbiferum).*

KEY FACTS

● **Name**
Turk's cap lily
(*Lilium superbum*)

● **Range**
Native to the eastern United States

● **Habitat**
Naturally occurs on moist slopes, marshes, and meadows that have acidic soil

● **Appearance**
Tall lily, reaching 3-10 ft (1-3 m) in height; bell-shaped flowers are orange, pink, or scarlet; inner surface of the flower covered in brown spots; six petal-like segments curved to form a turban-like shape; flowers 3-4 in (7.5-10 cm) wide, blooming from late July to early September; leafy stems; narrow leaves; scaly bulbs

● **Life cycle**
Perennial

● **Uses**
Ornamental

● **Status**
Common

Lime

◄ *Lime fruits. These fruits grow in clusters and have a tender, yellowish-green pulp.*

KEY FACTS

● **Name**
Lime tree
(*Citrus aurantifolia*)

● **Range**
Cultivated in tropical and warm temperate regions worldwide

● **Habitat**
Cultivated orchards

● **Appearance**
Small tree, reaching up to 16 ft (5 m) high; thorny branches, with short, stiff twigs; small leaves pale green in color; white flowers borne in clusters; globular or oval fruits are green and measure 1½-2½ in (3-6 cm) in diameter

● **Life cycle**
Perennial

● **Uses**
To add flavor and taste to food and drink; oil from rind and seeds used to make soap

● **Status**
Widespread in cultivation

In the eighteenth and nineteenth centuries, British sailors on long voyages often suffered from scurvy, a disease whose symptoms include bleeding gums and painful bones. Scurvy is caused by a lack of vitamin C, which is an essential part of a healthy human diet. The lime is a tree whose fruit is rich in vitamin C. As a result, the Royal Navy issued its men with limes to keep them healthy. "Limey" became a nickname for all British sailors.

The lime tree

The lime tree (*Citrus aurantifolia*) is a small, tropical evergreen. The group (genus) *Citrus* is made up of 16 species and is part of a large family of plants called the rue family (*Rutaceae*). The fruits of plants in this genus are commonly called citrus fruits and include the grapefruit (*Citrus paradisi*), lemon (*Citrus limonum*), and orange (*Citrus aurantium; Citrus sinensis*).

Limes are small trees, reaching no more than 16 ft (5 m) in height. Their spreading branches are irregular, with short, stiff twigs, small, pale-green leaves, and an abundance of small, sharp thorns. Due to their irregular growth, limes require regular pruning if they are not to become too bushy and dense.

Lime leaves are pale green in color. The tree bears small, white flowers in clusters. Lime fruits are green and typically measure about 1½-2½ in (3-6 cm) in diameter; they are oval or globular in shape. Lemons are larger and juicier than limes. Although they contain more sugar than lemons, many varieties of limes still taste just as sour.

A long history

Limes are thought to have originated in Southeast Asia and were probably introduced into Europe by crusaders returning from Palestine in the late twelfth and early thirteenth centuries. In 1493, explorer Christopher Columbus (1451-1506) took limes to the Americas on his second voyage. Lime trees took to the warm climate of Mexico, the southern United States, and the West Indies, and they soon became widely distributed throughout the Americas.

Many varieties

There are several different varieties of lime. The tropical West Indian lime – also called the Mexican lime or Key lime – has a small, seedy fruit. The seedless Persian or Tahiti lime is larger and grows mainly in subtropical regions. Both are extremely acidic limes. A less acidic, sweeter variety of lime is grown in Egypt and some tropical countries.

Uses of lime fruits

Limes are used mainly for their taste and flavor. The juice and zest is added to drinks and food such as sorbet and chutney (a spicy fruit pickle originating from India). Oil from the rind and seeds is used to make fragrant soaps.

Many people find limes too bitter to eat. However, limes may be crossed with different species to produce less acidic fruits. For example, crossing a kumquat and a lime produces a fruit called a limequat. These combined fruits are called hybrids and the process by which they are cultivated is called hybridization.

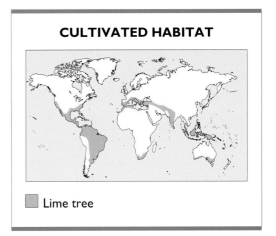

CULTIVATED HABITAT

Lime tree

A widely distributed fruit

Of all the citrus fruits, limes are the most susceptible to frost. As a result, limes are grown almost exclusively in tropical and warm temperate regions worldwide. Today most limes come from Brazil, which produces about 700,000 tons (635,000 tonnes) a year. Mexico produces the second-largest harvest, with over 500,000 tons (453,000 tonnes) annually. Other leading producers are the countries bordering the Mediterranean Sea, especially Italy and Spain, as well as Australia, South Africa, and the southern United States.

▼ *Lime trees (Citrus aurantifolia) are cultivated in tropical and warm temperate regions. Juice from their acidic fruits is used to flavor food and drink.*

Limpkin

The limpkin is a bird of freshwater swamps and marshes that is found from the southeastern United States to Argentina. It is the only living member of its family (the *Aramidae*), but it is closely related to the cranes and rails. Like the cranes the limpkin has long legs; the feet are not webbed but they have long toes with long claws, so the limpkin can walk over mud and swamp plants. The bill is long and downward curving like that of the Water rail and other long-billed rails.

Dependent on snails
The limpkin uses its powerful bill to pry water snails out of their shells. First it has to remove the horny protective shield (the operculum) that covers the opening. Then it places the snail on muddy ground with the opening in the shell facing upward. Grasping the shell firmly with the sharp claws of its foot, it removes the snail with its bill. The snail *Pomacea caliginosa* forms a major part of the diet and is so important a food that the limpkin cannot survive without it. Unlike the Snail kite, however, which feeds exclusively on snails, the limpkin does eat other prey such as crayfish, small reptiles, worms, and amphibians (frogs and toads).

▼ *The limpkin hunts in shallow water, finding shady places where there is lush vegetation. This bird is preening itself to clean its feathers.*

KEY FACTS

● **Name**
Limpkin
(*Aramus guarauna*)

● **Range**
From the southeastern states south through the West Indies to northern Argentina

● **Habitat**
Freshwater marshes and swamps

● **Appearance**
23-28 in (57-70 cm); dark brown flecked with white over the head, neck, and upperparts; a long, strong bill

● **Food**
Mainly freshwater snails, also worms, amphibians, crayfish, and small reptiles

● **Breeding**
Bulky nest of dried rushes and sticks built just above the water line in trees or bushes; 4-8 eggs; the young leave the nest the day they hatch

● **Status**
Widespread and common within its range; protected by law in parts of its range

The crying bird

The limpkin's method of hunting is to skulk along water edges, tail twitching. Often it moves along well-worn paths. This bird has a halting gait that makes it look as if it is limping, and this is what gives it the name "limpkin."

Although the limpkin is normally active during the daylight hours, where it has been persecuted it has become more wary, hunting at dusk and during the night. It is at these times especially that the bird's loud wailing call can be heard. The call has been likened to the cry of a baby, and in the southeastern United States this wailing sound is responsible for the limpkin's local name, the crying bird.

The limpkin rarely flies and when it does its flight is weak. It has a short takeoff and flies with its wings raised high over its back, its legs extended behind.

▲ *Although it spends most of its time at ground level, the limpkin can also be seen perching in trees and usually roosts in them at night.*

Where swamps and marshes have been drained, the water snail has disappeared and with it the limpkin. In parts of its range the limpkin is now protected by law. In wildlife sanctuaries in the U.S., notably Okefenokee Swamp in Georgia, the Everglades National Park, and Lake Okeechobee in Florida, the protection of habitats and species is showing results and the number of limpkins has increased.

Hunting has also caused a decline in the limpkin population. The flesh is reputedly very appetizing, so it has been hunted for food. The bird is by nature completely trusting of humans and so it is easy game.

NATURAL HABITAT

☐ Limpkin

See also **Crane, Kite, Snail, Wetland**

Lion

The lion is a beautiful and powerful cat. Often known as "The king of the beasts," the male of the species is truly majestic, with his bushy golden mane and loud, ferocious roar. In many cultures across the world, the lion is a symbol of strength, courage, and intelligence.

Prides to be proud of

Unlike other big cats, lions spend their time in large groups called prides. A pride may contain four to 12 related adult females and their cubs and one to six males. The males may also be related to each other, but not to the females.

Each pride has a territory that may extend 8-150 sq miles (20-400 km^2) and is defended fiercely by the males. If rival males come face to face, they will not normally resort to fighting but judge each other by their size, the loudness of their roars, and the bushiness of their manes. Every two or three years, however, the

males of a pride are confronted by rivals that are the same size or larger and stronger than they are. Then they will fight to the death, and the new leaders will take over the pride, often killing the cubs of the old leaders in the process.

The lion's share

In many ways, lions are the ultimate carnivores (meat eaters). They have large appetites: adult females need at least 10 lb (5 kg) of meat per day to survive, and adult males need 15 lb (7 kg). Therefore they have to be skilled hunters. Indeed, lions are perfectly adapted to killing, with their lean but muscular bodies, sharp, tearing claws, and short, powerful jaws. Their hearing and vision are excellent, and they stalk their prey under cover of night or in dense vegetation during the day.

Although lions share a range and type of prey with other carnivores such as

▲ *This lion's fine mane, which reaches down to his chest, shows that he is old and experienced.*

▶ *Females rear their young together. Many cubs die (up to 80 percent under the age of two), some through lack of food and some killed by male lions who take over a pride. This has the effect of making their mother ready to mate with the newcomers, ensuring that their offspring, and not those of other males, survive.*

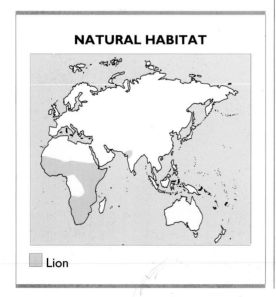

NATURAL HABITAT

Lion

leopards, wild dogs, and hyenas, they hunt the largest prey on the savannah and are the only predators that regularly catch and eat animals weighing up to 1100 lb (500 kg), including zebra, wildebeest, young giraffes, and buffalo. However, when larger prey is scarce they will eat almost anything that moves, targeting rodents, hares, small birds, and reptiles.

Despite the male lions' impressive size and ferocious image, the lionesses do most of the hunting. Unlike many cats, they are not solitary hunters, but prefer to hunt in teams, sometimes with up to 12 individuals at a time. They stalk their prey, creeping up on it stealthily and spreading out so that their victim is partially surrounded.

Once they are within about 100 ft (30 m) of the animal, one of the lionesses charges forward and seizes it or knocks it down with her huge paw. She then grabs it by the throat in her mighty jaws or holds its muzzle shut, effectively suffocating it. Once a kill is made, the whole pride shares the food, although the lionesses must wait for the larger and stronger male lions to take their fill first. However, when food is scarce, the lionesses may stop their cubs from eating, even if it means that they starve to death. Often lions will also steal the kill of other predators such as hyenas.

Looking after the cubs

Lions breed at any time of year, the lionesses mating with the males in their own pride. If there is more than one male, they do not fight for females. Whichever lion finds a willing female first becomes the dominant male of the pride. Three to four months after mating, the females give birth to a litter of one to five cubs. These are very small when they are born and weigh only about 4 lb (2 kg) – less than one percent of an adult's weight.

KEY FACTS

- **Name**
  Lion (*Panthera leo*)

- **Range**
  Africa, from the South Sahara down to South Africa; a small population in Northwest India

- **Habitat**
  Wooded grasslands, open savannah, semideserts

- **Appearance**
  Males measure up to $8\frac{1}{2}$-$10\frac{1}{2}$ ft (2.5-3 m) with a tail of 2-3 ft (60-90 cm); the coat is light tawny brown in color with white underparts; males have a large, bushy mane of reddish-brown or black fur

- **Food**
  Large and small mammals, small birds, reptiles

- **Breeding**
  Females have a litter of 1-5 cubs 3-4 months after mating; the cubs are very small and suckle (from their mother or other, related females) until they are 6 months old

- **Status**
  A subspecies, the Asiatic lion (*Panthera leo persica*) is endangered

See also **Leopard**

Lionfish

The lionfish is a dramatic and deadly inhabitant of the coral reefs of the tropical Indian Ocean and Western Pacific. It swims around the lagoons, usually in pairs or groups, in search of its prey that includes small fish, shrimp, and worms.

The lionfish is a member of the scorpion fish family, all of which have the most amazing arrangement of fins. The fins along the top of their backs (the dorsal fins) look rather like a row of flagpoles. They are made up of a series of spines with a small, fleshy area trailing behind each one.

Keep clear

The lionfish has vivid black, white, and pink, orange, or red coloring in stripy bands over its body and fins, which explains its other names – Dragon fish, Zebra fish, Butterfly fish, and Fire fish. However, the color and thorny shape of the fish are a warning to all to keep clear. The spines are not only sharp and sticky, but they also carry poisonous venom. They are hollow, so that the fish can actually inject the venom into its prey.

Anyone who brushes against one of these creatures certainly knows it because the spines cause sudden, sharp pain. If several spines dig into your flesh the effects can be disastrous: there may be a sudden rise and then a fall in body temperature, and in some cases the sting leads to heart failure and death.

Because it is so deadly, the lionfish has little to fear on the coral reefs where it lives. Few other fish attack it, so it can

KEY FACTS

- **Name**
  Lionfish, Dragon fish, Zebra fish, Butterfly fish, or Fire fish (*Pterois volitans*)

- **Range**
  Indian and western Pacific Oceans

- **Habitat**
  Coral reefs at depths of 25-130 ft (8-40 m)

- **Appearance**
  8-15 in (35-40 cm) long; spiny rayed fins with poisonous spikes; color ranges from pink to black, with white bands; a large broad head with a wide mouth; the body tapers toward the tail

- **Food**
  Small fish, shrimp, and worms

- **Breeding**
  Female lays eggs that are fertilized outside the body; no parental care

- **Status**
  Widespread

◄ *The lionfish has a large mouth that is low on its head for scooping up its prey.*

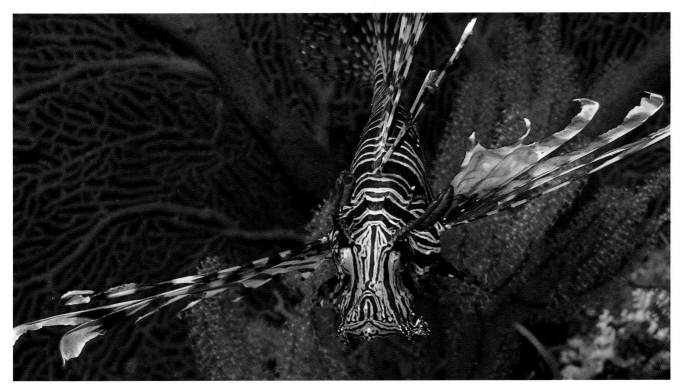

drift around in a lazy manner or lurk in holes or behind corals waiting for its next meal to drift past. Some related species spend much of the time relaxed, with dorsal, pectoral and pelvic fins close to its body. When the fish becomes annoyed, or when it is chasing prey, its spiny fins become erect, making it look very

ferocious. When the lionfish spots its prey it can move very rapidly, and it darts out to swallow smaller prey with one quick movement. It chases larger prey into a corner before attacking.

Deadly cousins

Other members of the *Pterois* genus look similar and share the many common names of the lionfish. The stonefish are also related. They are found in tropical waters and have the deadly weapons of the lionfish without their dramatic looks. Their spines are shorter, and they may half bury themselves in sand on the seabed where it is all too easy to tread on them. A single prick from the spines of some species may cause convulsions and lead to paralysis of the leg. These fish are frequently found along the northeastern coast of Australia, and hospitals in the area keep stocks of antivenom for emergencies.

▲ *The lionfish's pelvic and pectoral fins, around the lower part of the body, can be stretched out into huge fans, making it appear much larger than it is. These fins are used as a net to drive prey into corners of reefs where it can be eaten.*

NATURAL HABITAT

☐ Lionfish

See also **Coral reef**

Liverwort

If you were asked to imagine a plant, you might picture a small daffodil, a large, fragrant rose bush, or even a tall oak tree. Whichever plant you chose, chances are it would have leaves, roots, and perhaps flowers. However, some plants have none of

these features. Liverworts are tiny, green, plants in the class *Hepaticae* (also called *Marchantiophyta*). They get their name from an Old English word "wort," meaning plant or herb. Scientists called the plants liverworts because some species have a lobed- or liver-shaped form.

An ancient group of plants

Liverworts are among the most ancient groups of land plants around today. Liverworts have been around for about 400 million years, since the beginning of the Devonian Period.

Although botanists are not exactly sure, there are thought to be about 10,000 species of liverwort living throughout the world. They are common in moderately cool (temperate) and tropical regions. Like their cousins the mosses and hornworts (all these plants are collectively called bryophytes), liverworts are nonvascular plants. This means they do not have a

special system of tubes for transporting water and nutrients inside them, so they are extremely vulnerable to dehydration (loss of water). As a result, liverworts are usually found in moist or humid habitats, where they may grow on soil or the surfaces of trees or rocks.

Some liverworts, such as *Pellia epiphylla* and *Metzgeria furcata,* have a very simple structure. These species consist of just a thallus, which is a flattened and sometimes branching growth. Others, such as *Scapania nemorea* and *Radula complanata,* are a little more complex. They have leaf-like lobes arranged along a creeping shoot in two or three rows. The lobes in at least two of these ranks are usually overlapping and often folded. In some species, such as *Pleurozia purpurea,* they form small, water-holding pockets in which microscopic aquatic animals such as water fleas (*Daphnia* spp.) may live. Liverworts are anchored to the surface on

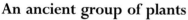

◄ **Marchantia polymorpha** *is found growing on damp soil in temperate regions worldwide. This liverwort reproduces asexually; that is, it can produce new plantlets without fertilization.*

KEY FACTS

- **Name**
  Marchantia polymorpha

- **Range**
  Moderately cool (temperate) regions worldwide

- **Habitat**
  Damp soil

- **Appearance**
  A flat, green thallus, which may be forked or lobed; thallus spreads out close to the ground

- **Life cycle**
  Sexual reproduction and vegetative reproduction by means of budding

- **Uses**
  None

- **Status**
  Widespread

which they live by delicate, thread-like structures called rhizoids. Unlike the roots that anchor most plants in the soil, rhizoids lack complex water-conducting tissues – each is only one cell thick.

Fungi associations

Some liverworts have a lifelong association with parasitic fungi. There is even one species, *Cryptothallus mirabilis,* that would become extinct if its close associate did not exist. *Cryptothallus mirabilis* does not contain green chlorophyll like other liverworts and so cannot provide its own food through photosynthesis (the process by which plants manufacture sugar). It is completely colorless, lives in the soil (often sheltering underneath mosses), and takes all its food from the fungus.

Liverwort life cycle

Like other nonflowering plants, liverworts have a complicated life cycle, consisting of two alternate stages – the gametophyte generation and the sporophyte generation. The gametophyte is the most familiar and persistent stage of the liverwort. It is also the stage when sexual reproduction occurs. Depending on the species, each gametophyte plant may be either male or female, or it may bear both male and female sex organs. Fertilization occurs in the presence of water. Because only the tiny male sex cells can move, they must swim from the male organs to reach and unite with the stationary female sex cells. Then the sporophyte generation develops from this fertilized cell.

Sporophytes are short-lived and, once mature, last only for a few days. During this stage, a special capsule develops. When it has fully matured, it rises above the thallus on a short, rapidly growing stalk. The capsule then splits into four segments, and thousands of tiny, seed-like spores are released into the air. The wind carries the spores far and wide, depositing them on the ground or in the crevices of a tree trunk or rock. The spores germinate and develop into gametophytes. The cycle begins again.

Vegetative reproduction

Some liverworts, such as *Marchantia polymorpha,* may reproduce vegetatively. This is a form of asexual reproduction where one plant produces new plantlets without fertilization. In this process, buds called gemmae (singular, gemma) break off and grow into new plants.

NATURAL HABITAT

Marchantia polymorpha

▼ *The spore-producing stage of a liverwort. The spores are held in the tiny capsule found on top of the short stalk. The mature capsule splits open and thousands of tiny spores are released and dispersed by the wind. Once they land, the spores germinate and develop into a sexually reproducing liverwort.*

Llama

The llama is one of the four species of the camel family that are found in the Andes Mountains of South America. The llama and its relative the alpaca are domestic animals that are closely related to the vicuna and the guanaco, the two wild camelids of the Andes. These four animals are sometimes known as the lamoids, to distinguish them from the camelids of Asia and Africa – the Bactrian camel and the dromedary.

Life at high altitudes
The llama lives in the grassy open spaces of the South American alpine plains. These plains occur at extremely high altitudes up to 15,700 ft (4250 m). The air is so thin that it contains 40 percent of the oxygen found in the air at sea level. The plains are also dry and cold and the soils are poor, so the grass is too tough for most grazing animals to digest.

The llamas and other camelids of the puna are perfectly adapted to these harsh conditions. They have thick, insulating wool coats, they are able to eat and digest the poor grasses, and they can take in more oxygen than other mammals at these heights. They also have padded feet that do not wear away the soil and a very particular way of moving (pacing), which means they can run very quickly and efficiently over the open plains.

Llama ancestors
There is a very strong association between the native people of the Andes (called the Incas) and the domestic lamoids. In fact the llama and the alpaca were domesticated by the mountain people around 4000-5000 years ago near Lake Titicaca (on the border between Bolivia and Peru). It is not known from exactly which species these animals

◄ *The Indians of the Andes domesticated llamas thousands of years ago. Llamas are no longer found in the wild.*

▲ *This llama is grazing the dry grasslands of the puna in Bolivia. Llamas may be any color from pure white to pitch black, with all the variations between the two, including gray and brown. The typical color, shown here, is brown. Spotted and dappled colorations are common and some animals are beautifully patterned.*

originated, but there are several theories. One theory is that llamas are domesticated guanacos and that alpacas are domesticated vicunas; another theory suggests that both are crosses between wild camelids; while a third theory says that the alpaca is a cross between the vicuna and the llama.

More than a pack animal

The llama is the largest of the South American camelids. It is used as a beast of burden and provides meat, fat for candles, hides for sandals, and dung for fuel.

There are two breeds of llama, the chaku, which has long hair that is mainly used for wool, and the cara, which is used for other resources. The pure white llama had an important religious significance for the Incas. It was chosen as the symbol of Inca royalty and was dressed with colorful shirts and decorated with gold earrings and collars of sea shells.

The alpaca

The alpaca, weighing 132 lb (60 kg), is only half the size of the llama and produces finer, very valuable wool. Like the llama its coat color varies, but coat pattern tends to be the same in all animals. The alpaca prefers the highest, most humid areas of the puna and is found mainly in Peru and Bolivia.

The guanaco occupies grasslands, scrub, and sometimes forests. It is found from sea level to the Andean foothills at heights of up to 13,900 ft (4250 m). The vicuna occupies the same regions as the llama.

Life in the herd

Llamas and alpacas usually graze in groups with one male and several females. The native people, making use of thousands of years of experience, manage their animals in these natural herd structures. The breeding season is in summer (from December to March) when the weather gets hotter and there is more rain. The calves can walk a few minutes after birth.

NATURAL HABITAT

Llama

See also **Camel, Mountain**

Lobster

More than 8,500 species of lobster are found throughout the seas of the world. They are particularly numerous in shallow waters around coasts. Most are about 12 in (30 cm) long. However, some species grow no bigger than a thumb, while others can grow to over 24 in (60 cm) and weigh over 45 lb (20 kg).

A segmented body

The adult lobster has a long body that is divided into 20 segments. The first five segments are all joined together and make up the head. The eyes are located on the ends of stalks and can be swiveled about. Below the eyes there is a pair of very long antennae. In some species these are longer than the body. They can be used as defensive weapons, as they are very tough and spiky.

The next eight segments make up the thorax, on which there are five pairs of legs. Lobsters are therefore classified with the crabs and shrimps in the group of

▲ *The North Atlantic lobster is the largest in the world. Its massive claws are capable of cutting off fingers. Lobsters continue to grow until they die. Some large specimens of lobster are over 50 years old and it is possible for them to live to 100 years of age.*

animals with ten legs, the *Decapoda* (from the Greek *deka*, meaning "ten" and *podos*, "legs"). Only four pairs of legs are used for walking over the seabed. In most species the first pair of legs have become claws.

The last six segments of the lobster's body make up the abdomen. Unlike the other segments, these are not fused together. The lobster can therefore curl its abdomen underneath its body. If the lobster does this quickly it pushes itself backward through the water at great speed – and it does this when escaping from enemies. On the underside of the abdomen are several paddle-like limbs called swimmerets that help the lobster move forward in the water. The male uses the first pair to carry sperm. The female uses hers to hold onto her eggs.

Life on the seabed

Lobsters are eaten by many creatures, including fish, humans, and even other lobsters. They spend their adult lives hidden away among corals or rocks, with only their long antennae showing. They only come out to mate or look for food. Lobsters eat a wide range of animal food, both living and dead. They shred their food into tiny pieces with their powerful jaws. Teeth in the

NATURAL HABITAT

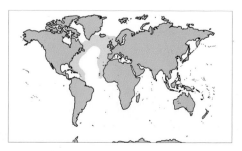

North Atlantic lobster

KEY FACTS

● **Name**
North Atlantic or
American lobster
(*Homarus americanus*)

● **Range**
Atlantic Ocean

● **Habitat**
The seabed among
rocks and corals

● **Appearance**
Up to 24 in (60 cm);
heavily built with an
armored body and
limbs; 8 crawling legs
and 2 fat claws; long
antennae

● **Food**
Other sea creatures,
either dead or alive

● **Breeding**
Female carries the
eggs until they hatch;
the larvae float,
feeding on smaller
animals; they then
crawl on the seabed
like adults; can take
two or more years
to reach adulthood

● **Status**
Becoming more rare
as they are exploited
for food

▶ *The Spiny lobster
(this one lives in the
Caribbean) is
becoming rare because
too many are being
caught for food.*

lobster's stomach help break down hard substances such as pieces of shell.

If a lobster is attacked it can protect itself in a number of ways. Lobsters with large claws can use them to grab an attacker, cutting deep into its flesh. They will not let go until the attacker retreats or the lobster itself is killed. Clawless lobsters use their long spiky antennae to protect themselves. They can keep two fish at bay, one on either side of their body. Some antennae have sharp jagged edges that can slice through skin.

Lobster life cycle

Female lobsters can produce anything from a few hundred to over 100,000 eggs at a time, depending on age and species. The eggs are small and pink, turning darker when they are ready to hatch.

The female lobster does not take care of the newly hatched larvae (young); she allows them to float away on the tide. There are two main types of lobster larvae. Those of the clawed lobsters look like tiny transparent shrimp with long legs. The larvae of the clawless lobsters are flat and leaf-like and are also transparent. Both types spend the first week or so of their lives swimming near the surface of the sea. They feed on microscopic plants and animals. Very few larvae reach the next stage in their development. Most are eaten by predators.

As they grow the larvae shed their external skeletons and develop new ones as many as ten or more times. Once this process has been completed, they swim down to the seabed. By now they look more like their parents. However, it will be several years before they mate.

Some species migrate after mating to areas more suitable for their offspring. However, some migrate for other reasons. For example, the clawless spiny lobsters migrate in vast numbers from shallow water to deeper water during the winter months. Each lobster follows directly behind the lobster in front because visibility in the water is sometimes very poor. These "lobsters trains" can stretch for some 300 yards (275 m).

537

Loon

The loons are a unique group of birds renowned among other things for their handsome appearance and haunting cries. They are highly regarded not only by naturalists and bird watchers but by most people who have had the chance to see them in their natural habitat. In the summer the birds take up residence on the thousands of lakes in the northern forests and on the stretches of water that lie in the desolate open country of the tundra. In the fall they migrate, most of them spending the winter on the coasts.

There are five living species of loon, all of which belong to the same group (the genus *Gavia*). They have streamlined bodies shaped like torpedoes, straight, pointed bills, and fairly long, stout necks. Their tails are very short and almost disappear into the line of the body. In their winter feathers the species look so much alike that even experts can have difficulty telling them apart. They are sooty gray above with bars of lighter gray and white below. All five species – the Common loon, the Arctic loon, the Red-throated loon, the Pacific loon, and the Yellow-billed loon – are found in North America, as well as in Europe and Asia.

Highly specialized

The loons are excellent divers and swimmers. When they are alarmed they will disappear below the surface of the water in a flash – they are there on the water one minute but gone the next. Taken movement by movement, the loon begins its dive by arching its neck and pointing its bill downward. Then it gives a forceful thrust with its powerful webbed feet to propel itself into the water. When the loon is swimming below the surface it uses its feet to drive itself through the water. The narrow tapering wings help in balancing and turning.

Loons dive for fish and other aquatic animals living in shallow waters. When hunting they usually remain submerged for only 30-40 seconds. Yet records show that these birds can dive to depths of 240 ft (73 m) and can stay below the surface for eight minutes, swimming a distance of 300-400 yards (274-366 m) in that time.

▼ *Young loons are ready to leave the nest the day after hatching and can swim and dive well after 10-13 days. For the first couple of weeks, parents often carry the young on their backs.*

KEY FACTS

● **Name**
Common loon or
Great northern diver
(*Gavia immer*)

● **Range**
Canada, Iceland,
Greenland, and the
coast of northwest
Europe; winters on
the Great Lakes and
along the coasts of
the Pacific, Atlantic,
and Gulf of Mexico

● **Habitat**
Lakes and coasts

● **Appearance**
27-37 in (68-81 cm);
heavy head, short,
stout neck, and long
body; swims low in
the water; in the
summer the head and
neck are glossy black,
the back is black with
broad flecks, the
underparts are white;
in the winter the
head, neck, and
upperparts are dark
gray or brown, the
cheeks, throat, and
underparts white

● **Food**
Fish, crustaceans,
insects, amphibians

● **Breeding**
Both parents build a
nest of matted grass
and twigs; 1-3 eggs
are laid May-June

● **Status**
Common

▲ *The sleek feathers act as waterproofing for loons like this Red-throated loon. It holds its neck curved back against its body when it is sitting or swimming, only straightening it to dive or fly.*

The loon not only dives well, it can also submerge itself below the surface of the water while in a "sitting" position. By expelling air from its feathers and from an air sac inside its body, it slowly slides underwater with only a few ripples to show where it was swimming.

The loon is one of the only birds in which most of the leg is contained within the body. Only the portion below the ankle can be seen on the outside. The legs are also positioned well back toward the tail. These features make it difficult for the loon to walk on land and it shambles along very slowly and awkwardly, taking only a few steps at a time. Its clumsy movement on land is responsible for the bird's common name, loon, which comes from a Scandinavian word *lom*, meaning lame. In many parts of the world they are called divers.

In spite of a heavy body, loons are strong fliers, often reaching an air speed of 60 mph (96 km/h). However, they cannot take off from land and even have trouble taking off on water. They have to "run" across the surface of the water for 60 ft (18 m) or more before taking flight.

NATURAL HABITAT

Common loon

Lungfish

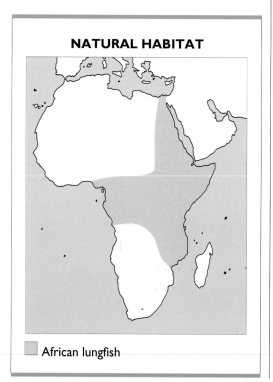

NATURAL HABITAT

African lungfish

▲ *The rare Australian or Queensland lungfish* (**Neoceratodus forsteri**) *is an eel-like creature. Like other lungfish, it preys on small fish.*

The lungfish is an ancient freshwater fish that was very common in all parts of the world some 350-400 million years ago. Today there are only six living species: four in Africa, one in South America, and one in Australia. All of them have lungs for taking in oxygen from the air. They also have gills for taking in oxygen from the water like most fish.

Breathing at the surface

The lungfish's swim bladder (the organ that allows the fish to stay at a particular depth of water) has been converted into lungs that work in much the same way as human lungs. The fish uses its gills when under water, but every once in a while it swims to the surface and gulps in some air. The South American lungfish, for example, comes to the surface at regular intervals of about one minute. African

KEY FACTS

● **Name**
African lungfish (*Protopterus aethiopicus*)

● **Range**
Rivers and lakes of eastern and central Africa

● **Habitat**
Shallow waters, muddy riverbeds

● **Appearance**
$6\frac{1}{2}$ ft (2 m) long; dark gray above, heavily mottled; yellowish-gray or pink below; a long, eel-like body flattened at the tail end; trailing pectoral and pelvic fins

● **Food**
Fish, crustaceans, mollusks

● **Breeding**
The male makes a burrow in which the female lays her eggs; both the eggs and young are guarded by the male; the young have external gills, then develop adult gills and lungs when they are about $1\frac{1}{2}$ in (4 cm) long

● **Status**
Widespread

540

lungfish have to come to the surface at least once every half hour.

A fish that has lungs has a great advantage over other fish. If the water it lives in is rather stagnant (lacking in oxygen and therefore foul) the lungfish can still get all the oxygen it needs. Also, if the pond, swamp, or lake dries up the fish may still survive.

Survival out of water

With the exception of the Australian species, all the lungfish are able to live without water for certain periods of time if it gets very hot and dry. They go into a resting state, called aestivation, that is similar to the state of hibernation that some animals in cold climates undergo in winter.

In times of drought the lungfish burrows into the mud at the bottom of the waterhole or lake and curls up with its tail around its head. It then secretes a lot of of slimy mucus that fills up the burrow and almost completely surrounds the fish like a cocoon. A small hole remains just by the fish's mouth, allowing air to pass through. As the heat of the sun dries the mud, the mucus hardens into a capsule. This prevents the fish from dying of dehydration.

In most cases the resting period lasts for several weeks. During this time the fish breathes more slowly than normal and it uses its own muscles for food. When the

▲ *Beneath the mud on dried-up riverbeds and lakes, the African lungfish may go into a dormant state. Its long body is curled up into an oval shape, and it may remain like this, protected by mucus, for several years.*

rains come and the lakes and pools fill with water the fish returns to a free-swimming life; the rain makes the ground muddy, the capsule dissolves, and the fish swims away. However there are records of lungfish surviving in their underground capsules for four years. Although they were extremely thin when they came out, they did not suffer any other ill effects from their long sleep.

The Australian lungfish does not aestivate and, if the rivers and pools in which it lives dry up, this fish cannot survive. Some lungfish (such as the African species *Protopterus aethiopicus*) live in large lakes that are permanently filled with water. Although these lungfish can aestivate, they normally do not have to.

Protecting the young

In both the South American and African lungfish the breeding season begins at the start of the rainy season. The male digs a depression in the mud and here the female deposits up to 5000 eggs. The male looks after the eggs, protecting them from predators who come near. He also oxygenates the water around them by wiggling his body so that currents of water wash over the eggs.

The male continues his protective role after the eggs have hatched. The young are dark brown to black in color and are able to breathe air when they are about $1^1/_2$ in (4 cm) long.

Lynx

The lynx is a heavy, bushy cat with a soft thick coat that gives it a "padded" appearance. It is related to other small cats such as the domestic cat and the ocelot, but it is most often confused with the bobcat. However, it is usually larger than the bobcat, with more pronounced ear and cheek tufts and longer legs.

A cold existence

The lynx is a shy animal that is nocturnal (active at night) and spends its time alone rather than in groups. During the day the lynx rests, sleeping in trees or in comfortable hollows on rocky outcrops. At dusk it stirs, venturing out in search of food. It is a carnivore (meat eater) and preys on small animals such as hares (in North America, the Snowshoe hare makes up most of its diet), ground-dwelling birds such as grouse, foxes, and young deer.

In the poor light, the lynx is well camouflaged; its brownish-gray fur with soft markings allows it to blend in with the background of rocks, vegetation, and conifer trees that cover most of its range.

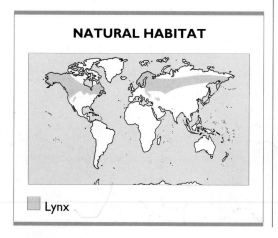

NATURAL HABITAT

▨ Lynx

As the lynx hunts its prey it creeps along stealthily, making no noise with its soft, padded paws. It uses its excellent hearing to detect its victims moving in the undergrowth and its exceptional sense of smell to identify animals some distance away. Alternatively, it may lie quietly in the undergrowth or on a low tree branch, waiting for its unlucky victim to pass by. Then, as soon as the animal is close

▲ *Some scientists believe that the lynx's long, characteristic ear tufts (like those of the Canadian lynx shown here) somehow improve their excellent hearing.*

enough, it leaps out in attack, shocking its prey – it has even been known to leap high in the air to catch birds as they try to fly away. Once it has caught an animal, it grips it tightly with its sharp claws and gives it a fatal bite to the neck.

Separate home ranges

Males and females have separate territories, which they mark with urine and feces. However, during the mating season, which starts in the spring, the male lynx leaves his territory to travel in search of a mate, fighting fiercely with rival males along the way.

The female lynx gives birth to a litter of 1-5 cubs about two months after mating. These are born in a special den hidden in an outcrop of rocks or a hollow tree. The cubs are blind and helpless when they are born, although they open their eyes within 10 days and are able to explore the outside world at five weeks. Their mother suckles them until they are about five months old. They stay with her until the following spring, when they have developed the hunting skills they need to survive on their own.

The caracal

As well as the bobcat, there is another small cat that is closely related to the lynx. The caracal (*Felis caracal*) is an animal that inhabits the dry grassland and savannah in parts of Africa, Arabia, southwest Asia, Turkestan, and India. It is usually lighter than the lynx, weighing up to 50 lb (23 kg).

The caracal's coat is much smoother and less bushy than that of the lynx, and the color varies from sandy to reddish-brown without markings. However, it does have the characteristic long, dark ear tufts – indeed, its name comes from the Turkish word *karakal*, meaning "black ear."

▼ *This European lynx has large, round feet covered in thick fur and a dense, fluffy coat that protects it from the bitter winter weather, when temperatures may drop as low as -70°F (-57°C).*

KEY FACTS

● **Name**
Lynx *(Felis lynx)*

● **Range**
Alaska, Canada, northern U.S., northern Eurasia, parts of southern Europe

● **Habitat**
Coniferous forest, scrub, tundra

● **Appearance**
A medium-sized cat, with a head and body length of 2-3½ ft (0.5-1 m) and a short tail of 2-5½ in (5-14 cm); a thick, soft coat, varing in color, often a grayish-brown with dark markings; the tail has a dark tip and the cheeks and ears have long, black tufts

● **Food**
Mainly hares but also foxes, rodents, ground-dwelling birds, and young deer

● **Breeding**
One litter per year, containing 1-5 cubs; the cubs are weaned at 5 months and stay with their mother for their first winter

● **Status**
Widespread, but the Spanish lynx *(Felis lynx pardina)* is endangered

See also **Bobcat**

Macaw

▲ *The large head and beak of the macaw is balanced by its long tapering tail. This pair of Blue-and-yellow macaws (Ara ararauna), spying out the land from an old tree trunk, are showing their perching and creeping skills.*

Macaws are a group of parrots found in the tropical jungles of South and Central America. They are the largest of the parrots, with long, elegant tails that are often more than half the total length of the bird. The world's largest parrot is the Hyacinth macaw (*Anodorhynchus hyacinthinus*), with a total length of 40 in (1 m), which is found in tropical eastern Brazil and Bolivia. Other colorful species include the Red-and-green macaw and the Blue-and-yellow macaw. They are all renowned for their brilliant coloring and are often seen in zoos or kept as pets – and they make very good companions.

Flocking and feeding

These colorful birds can be seen flashing through the canopy of the rainforest, where they need strong coloring to attract a mate. They are very sociable birds, often gathering together in large groups to sleep and, in the morning, flying off to feeding grounds nearby.

Parrots build up close relationships with their partners, and are seen flying close together in pairs or in larger family groups. Sometimes the groups number over 50. They communicate to each other with harsh, noisy squawks, and, if they are disturbed in their feeding ground, take to the air together as soon as they hear a warning call.

Parrots' beaks have a distinctive shape, with hooked upper beaks that fit neatly over their lower beaks. They are very powerful: they use the hooked upper beak to tear at fruit, and they crush hard seeds and nutshells between their jaws at the back of their mouths.

Their feet are also adapted to help them find and eat their favorite foods. When they perch on a branch, if you look at them from the front they look as though they have only two toes. Two other toes are at the back of the foot, gripping the perch tightly. However, if they need to they can use one foot to grip food and lift it to their mouth. In the restricted spaces of the tropical rainforests, they can be seen climbing branches, using both beak and feet to claw their way along.

Human relationships

Little is known about the breeding habits of these birds because they live in very inaccessible parts of the Amazon Basin. They build their nests in tall trees, or

NATURAL HABITAT

Red-and-green macaw

sometimes in crevices in rock faces. It is known that they form very strong bonds, and even if they are members of a flock, the male and female keep together within the flock. They show great devotion to both their mate and their offspring and, in captivity, they often transfer this affection to a human friend.

However, the attractive appearance and friendly nature of macaws, coupled with the constant invasion of their tropical habitat by humans, means that their numbers are falling. Although only three species (the Glaucous, Indigo, and Little blue macaws) are listed as endangered, the last of these, also known as Spix's Macaw (*Cyanopsitta spixii*), has been illegally trapped and is now on the brink of extinction. It comes from a remote region of northeastern Brazil. The only hope for the species lies with the few individuals that are held in captivity.

◄ *Like other species of macaw, the Red-and-green macaw uses its heavy beak to crack open nuts. Its favorites are Brazil nuts. It also eats a wide range of fruit in the humid, lowland forests.*

KEY FACTS

● **Name**
Red-and-green or Green-winged macaw (*Ara chloropterus*)

● **Range**
Eastern Panama to Brazil and northern Argentina

● **Habitat**
Humid forest

● **Appearance**
Length 36 in (90 cm); mainly red, with red, blue, and green wings

● **Food**
Large fruit and nuts (including Brazil nuts)

● **Breeding**
Nests in a hollow high up in a tall tree or in crevices in cliffs; two eggs are laid

● **Status**
Becoming rare; numbers have declined due to habitat loss and hunting and trapping

See also **Brazil nut tree, Parrot, Rainforest**

Magnolia

The sweet-smelling magnolia is grown around the world for its beautiful leaves and flowers. The magnolia is named after Pierre Magnol (1638-1715), professor of botany at Montpellier University, France.

Where do they grow?

The group (genus) *Magnolia* is made up of about 100 species of trees and shrubs and, along with six other groups, belongs to the *Magnoliaceae* family. About 80 percent of this family is native to tropical Southeast Asia, from the Himalayas eastward to Indonesia, Japan, and the Philippines. The remainder is native to North and Central America, Venezuela in South America, and the Caribbean. However, their popularity as ornamental

▲ *The creamy-white petals of the flower of the Southern magnolia or Bull bay (**Magnolia grandiflora**). This flower is made up of 12 delicate petals arranged in three layers of four. The male and female reproductive organs are in the center of the flower.*

plants in gardens and parks means that plants from this family are now cultivated all over the world.

Plant parts

The leaves of magnolias are very handsome, with striking symmetrical shapes and a shiny or leathery appearance. Some species are evergreen, which means their leaves stay green and last for more than one growing season. Others are deciduous, which means that they shed their leaves in the fall.

However, magnolias are best known for their large and beautifully scented pink, purple, white, or yellow flowers. Each flower has three sepals. The sepals are tiny modified leaves that enclose the flower in a bud and open around the base of the flower when it blooms. Between six and 12 petals form two, three, or four whorls, which, in turn, surround numerous spirally arranged stamens (male pollen-producing structures).

NATURAL HABITAT

☐ Southern magnolia

▶ *A cone-like structure
consisting of many
fruits (called follicles)
develops following
fertilization of the
flowers of the Southern
magnolia. Red seeds
hang from the fruits by
slender threads.*

Following pollination and fertilization of the female reproductive cells, contained within the ovaries, the fruits develop in a cone-shaped structure.

Follicle fruits

Magnolia seeds are usually red. The seeds often hang by slender threads from the cone-like fruiting structure, which consists of many small, dry fruits called follicles. One or two seeds are contained in each follicle. The outer coat of each seed becomes fleshy and red as the fruit ripens. When the follicle splits open, the seed dangles from it by the slender thread.

Shapes and sizes

Many magnolias are popularly grown as ornamental trees and shrubs; others are

important sources of building timber. Umbrella trees (*Magnolia tripetala*) grow to heights of about 40 ft (12 m). They get their name from their vast leaves, which are typically about 2-ft- (0.6-m-) long and so can be used as umbrellas.

Among the more popular species native to North America are the Southern magnolia, the Sweet bay magnolia, and the Cucumber tree.

The Southern magnolia, Bull bay, or Laural bay (*Magnolia grandiflora*) is found from North Carolina through Florida and around the Gulf coast to eastern Texas. In its natural habitat this evergreen tree can reach heights of between 80 and 100 ft (24 and 30 m). Its creamy-white flowers grow at the ends of the tree's branches and are surrounded by thick, leathery, oval-shaped leaves up to 10 in (25 cm) long. The flowers are highly scented and measure between 6 and 9 in (15 and 23 cm) when fully open. The flowers are so attractive that the plant is cultivated as an ornamental in most warm temperate regions of the world.

The Sweet bay magnolia (*Magnolia virginiana*) is found in moist regions from Massachusetts to Texas. It grows to about 60 ft (18 m) in height and is evergreen in the south but deciduous in the north of the areas in which it is found.

The Cucumber tree (*Magnolia acuminata*) is found in the open woodlands in the Appalachian region, Ozark Mountains, and Ohio and Mississippi river valleys. This deciduous magnolia can grow up to 100 ft (30 m) high. The plant takes its name from its cucumber-shaped fruits, which may grow up to 3 in (7.5 cm) long.

Manatee

The manatee is an unusual, slow-moving sea mammal that never leaves the water. Like its cousin, the dugong, the manatee is huge and lumbering and is often referred to as the "sea cow;" the Portuguese also call it the "fish cow." It belongs to the small group of sea mammals known as the sirenians (*Sirenia*).

The living sirenians include the dugong and three species of manatee – the North American (also known as the West Indian), the South American or Amazonian, and the West African manatee. One other species, Steller's sea cow (*Hydrodamalis gigas*), was hunted to the brink of extinction by whalers and sealers in the middle of the eighteenth century. Later it died out completely.

The manatee's body is rather similar to that of the dugong. It is fish-shaped, up to 15 ft (4.5 m) long, and has paddle-like forelimbs, or flippers. It has a broad, rounded tail, which it holds horizontally, and its mouth has a split upper lip fringed

NATURAL HABITAT

☐ North American manatee

with bristles. Its face is creased and hairy, but the remaining parts of the body are smooth and hairless.

Peaceful vegetarians

The manatee is sluggish and easy going. It spends much of its time resting at the surface of the water with only its back visible. It can remain submerged for up to ten minutes at a time before it has to raise its head to breathe. Sometimes in shallow water it rests in an upright position, its tail tucked under its body and its head and shoulders out of the water.

Manatees are active mainly at night. They eat only plant material, feeding mostly on marine vegetation such as eelgrass and seaweeds. They often forage in the mud of the seabed and feed on the rhizomes (underground stems) of sea grasses. Occasionally, however, they will pluck leaves from land plants that are overhanging the water.

▲ *Despite being so large and lumbering, the manatee's body is surprisingly streamlined, almost like that of a fish. We can see in this picture of a North American manatee (Trichechus manatus) how the rounded tail is large and powerful. The small forelimbs are mainly used for paddling and steering.*

The manatee's split upper lip is very mobile. The two halves are used like a grasping tool to pick up plants – each half of the lip can be moved separately from the other half. It is thought that the bristles help to push the food into the manatee's mouth.

Baby sea cows

North American manatees appear to mate at any time of the year, when a group of 5-17 males will congregate around a receptive female, pushing and shoving each other in order to establish which of them will mate with her. It is thought that the female may be ready to mate for several weeks, and she mates with more than one male within that time.

Up to 12 months after mating, the female gives birth to a single calf. Immediately after it is born, the calf rides on its mother's back. Then its mother slowly begins to submerge until eventually the calf is swimming freely. The mother suckles the calf for a long period – 12-18 months – although it begins to eat plant material when it is a few weeks old.

Manatees under threat

All three species of manatee are under threat of extinction. In Florida, for example, the North American manatee almost died out, but it has been protected in this area since the enlargement of the Everglades National Park in 1950. However, many animals still die from the injuries they receive when they collide with the outboard motors of small boats and, in South American waters, from hunting. The manatee has traditionally been killed for its appetizing flesh in many parts of South America and this practice continues despite current protection.

▼ *Unlike the North American or West African manatees, the South American manatee (below) is only found in fresh water. It lives in lakes and rivers, where it feeds at the surface.*

KEY FACTS

● **Name**
North American or West Indian manatee (*Trichechus manatus*)

● **Range**
Waters of southeastern North America, through the Caribbean, and south to Brazil

● **Habitat**
Seawater and fresh water of coasts and coastal rivers in warm areas; muddy estuaries

● **Appearance**
Large body, dark gray to blackish, up to 15 ft (4.5 m) long, and weighing 3527 lb (1600 kg); a thick, cleft lip with tough bristles, small eyes, 2 forelimbs, a broad tail shaped like a paddle

● **Food**
Floating sea plants, some land plants, and freshwater plants from rivers and lakes

● **Breeding**
Single young, born every two years at any time of year; the calf weighs 40 lb (18 kg) at birth, suckled for 12-18 months

● **Status**
Endangered

See also **Dugong, Ocean**

Mandrill

A brightly colored mask

As is the case with many mammals, the male mandrill is the most recognizable sex, with its vivid scarlet and blue face and rump. The colors of this "mask" may become more intense whenever the animal is angry or alarmed. They also become brighter and stronger with age, so that the oldest, strongest, and most experienced baboons are easily distinguished, discouraging competition from rivals.

This may also be the reason for the bright colors on the rump, although some scientists think that this also serves as a visual signal for the group, so that they can keep track of each other in the dark rainforests of western Central Africa.

Living in troops

Like other baboons, mandrills are very sociable, living in large groups known as troops. These contain at least one adult male and several females with their offspring and may have up to 200 members altogether. Each troop has a home range of about 30 sq miles (50 km²). Mandrills are diurnal animals (active during the day) and spend the night asleep high in the branches of trees where they are safer from predators.

Soon after sunrise, the mandrills wake up and become active, the whole troop following the dominant adult male, who decides where the troop will feed that day. Throughout the day, the troop may cover 5 miles (8 km), foraging for food and keeping in contact with each other

The mandrill is the biggest monkey in the world. A male may measure up to 32 in (82 cm) and weigh as much as 110 lb (50 kg), although the female is usually half this size. It is a fierce-looking baboon, with a long, dog-like muzzle and large teeth. However, despite its ferocious appearance, the mandrill is actually a relatively shy animal, and its characteristic teeth-baring expression usually indicates friendliness rather than rage.

▲ *This male mandrill's face is almost like a brightly colored mask. It is used to impress and intimidate rivals and intruders of a lower rank.*

KEY FACTS

● **Name**
Mandrill
(Papio sphinx)

● **Range**
Central Africa

● **Habitat**
Dense rainforest

● **Appearance**
Large, robust
baboon, males
measuring up to 27 in
(70 cm), with a tail of
4$\frac{1}{2}$ in (12 cm); the
hairless face is very
long and marked with
deep ridges, vividly
colored red and blue
in the case of males
(as is the rump); the
females and offspring
are duller in color;
olive brown on the
upperparts and
flanks, and grayish-
yellow on the
underparts with a
yellow-orange beard

● **Food**
Fruit, roots, seeds,
leaves, insects,
worms, eggs, some
small mammals

● **Breeding**
Females give birth to
1 young, about 7$\frac{1}{2}$
months after mating
with the dominant
male; the young
baboon suckles for
about 8 months

● **Status**
Endangered

with a range of calls that echo through the dense rainforest. These may become louder and shriller, sounding the alarm if there is danger from predators.

Mandrills are mainly vegetarian, eating a range of leaves, roots, seeds, and fruit, although from time to time they may also feed on insects, worms, eggs, and even small mammals. Like other monkeys, mandrills have very long arms and hands that can grasp tightly. They sometimes climb trees to find the best fruit, although they are most often seen on the ground, standing on three limbs and using one hand to sort through the vegetation and lift the food to their mouths. When they are not feeding, they rest in their groups, the adults grooming each other and the offspring playing games.

Young baboons

Once they are about four years old, the females are able to mate and, once every 33 days, their rumps swell to indicate when they are ready. All the females in the troop usually mate with the dominant male. About 7$\frac{1}{2}$ months after mating, a single young is born. The baby mandrill is fairly well developed at birth, with a thin covering of fur and open eyes. Its coloring is the same as that of its mother – a dull olive brown, with very faint, blue tinges on its face. Its hands are able to grasp, and it clings tightly to its mother's chest, already able to support its own weight.

Once it is eight months old, the young baboon is weaned, although it has already been eating some solid food for two or three months. It stays with its mother for about two years and then becomes

▲ *This male mandrill in shallow water stands in the typical baboon posture, on all fours with the shoulders slightly higher than the hips.*

independent, although it remains within the same group as its parents. Females stay within this group, but once young males have reached the age of four to six years, they have developed their bright coloring and are chased away by the dominant male, who may regard them as rivals.

NATURAL HABITAT

Mandrill

See also **Baboon**

Mangrove

Tropical swamps, such as those in the Florida Everglades, often contain dense thickets or even forests of mangrove. This extraordinary evergreen is an easy tree to recognize. In addition to having a central trunk growing out of the ground, it has adapted to its muddy environment by developing structures called "aerial roots." These roots grow from the trunk back down into the swamp to give the

▲ *The roots of the Red mangrove are exposed and visible at low tide. They give the tree added support and allow those roots buried beneath the mud to breathe.*

tree added support. Aerial roots are also known as prop or stilt roots.

The Red mangrove

The mangrove family (*Rhizophoraceae*) contains about 15 groups (genera) and 120 different kinds (species). They are found in tropical regions all over the world. The genus *Rhizophora* contains about eight or nine species, including the Red, or American, mangrove (*Rhizophora mangle*). This mangrove is found across southern Florida and the West Indies, into South America, and along the Atlantic coast of Africa. In Florida, the Red mangrove rarely exceeds 20 ft (6 m) in height; elsewhere it may grow 100 ft (30 m) high, with a trunk diameter of up to 3 ft (1 m).

The Red mangrove has long, leathery, oval-shaped leaves and pale-yellow flowers. Following pollination and fertilization, the flowers mature into brownish berries up to about 1⅓ in (0.3 cm) long. The berries begin to germinate while on the parent mangrove tree, sending out a 12 in (30 cm) root. When the fruit drops from the tree, the root is either driven into the mud or else the fruit floats until it contacts a muddy surface. As soon as the root embeds itself in the mud, it begins to grow.

The dense, hard, red-colored wood that gives the Red mangrove its name is often used for fuel and in construction. The thick, gray or grayish-red bark is an important source of tannin, which is used to tan leather, dye fabrics, and make ink.

NATURAL HABITAT

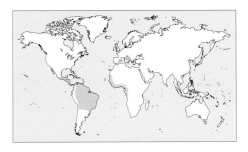

■ Red mangrove

The root of the matter

Mangrove roots are typically covered by water at high tide but become exposed and visible at low tide. The roots of many mangrove species project above the mud and have small breathing pores through which air enters. Once inside the roots, the air passes through a soft, spongy tissue and down into those roots lying beneath the mud. This adaptation allows the covered roots to breathe while growing in waterlogged soil.

The exposed aerial roots of the Red mangrove form tangled thickets that catch and hold debris, soil, and other organic material. As a result, large mangrove forests in coastal regions may help to stabilize and slowly extend the shoreline.

Tenants and visitors

Some of the animals and plants that inhabit mangrove forests are as amazing and unusual as the tree itself. Mangroves are the sole breeding ground of the tsetse fly (*Glossina* spp.), an African insect which carries parasites of the genus *Trypanosoma*. These parasites can cause sleeping sickness in both humans and domestic animals. Fully grown tsetse larvae, born singly at intervals of about 10 to 15 days, are deposited in mangrove roots where soils are moist and loose.

Mangroves are also homes to Spanish mosses or graybeards (*Tillandsia usneoides*). Spanish moss is not a true moss but belongs to the pineapple family (*Bromeliaceae*) and grows on trees and rocks. Each stem of the moss bears thread-like leaves and small, green or blue flowers. It may hang from mangrove branches in strands over 20 ft (6 m) long.

◄ *The Red mangrove's berries produce roots while still on the tree.*

KEY FACTS

● **Name**
Red mangrove
(*Rhizophora mangle*)

● **Range**
Southern Florida and the West Indies, into South America, and along the Atlantic coast of Africa

● **Habitat**
Dense thickets or even forests in warm, muddy salt water along tidal estuaries, marshes, or coasts

● **Appearance**
In Florida, Red mangroves can be 20 ft (6 m) high; tropical Red mangroves can be 100 ft (30 m) high; long, leathery, oval-shaped leaves, pale-yellow flowers, and brownish berries

● **Life cycle**
Perennial

● **Uses**
Fuel; tannin for making ink, dyeing fabrics, and tanning leather; timber

● **Status**
Common and widespread

See also **Bromeliad, Tide pool and coast, Wetland**

Maple

◀ *The leaves of the Sugar maple (Acer saccharum) turn a beautiful bronze color in the fall.*

Maples are trees and shrubs that belong to the maple family (*Aceraceae*). This family consists of two groups (genera) – *Acer* and *Dipteronia* – and 113 different kinds (species). Maples are found throughout the eastern part of Canada; they are also widely distributed across other parts of the northern hemisphere in countries with moderately cool (temperate) climates. Maples are particularly common in China, Japan, and the United States.

Shade trees and ornamentals

Many maple trees have beautifully colored leaves. Their spreading branches make maples popular as shade trees and ornamentals – trees that are planted as decoration in large gardens, parks, and along roadsides. The Norway maple (*Acer platanoides*) is one such tree. In the wild, it bears greenish-yellow flower clusters in the spring. However, varieties with bronze, maroon, purple, or red flowers have been developed through selective breeding. Selective breeding is a process by which plants are grown for specific characteristics such as color, shape, or size.

Nearly all maples are deciduous, which means that they shed their leaves in the fall. However, a few species – for example, the Cretan maple (*Acer sempervirens*) – are evergreen.

The leaves of some maples are deeply indented into three or more lobes with distinctive, tooth-like edges. Across the genus, however, the leaves are highly

KEY FACTS

● **Name**
Red maple (*Acer rubrum*)

● **Range**
Moderately cool (temperate) zones from southeastern Canada to Texas and Florida

● **Habitat**
Occurs in all types of habitat

● **Appearance**
Trees up to 120 ft (37 m) tall, with spreading branches; trunk 5 ft (1.5 m) in diameter; leaves measure 2 to 6 in (5 to 15 cm) across with five tooth-edged lobes; leaves turn deep red in the fall

● **Life cycle**
Perennial

● **Uses**
Ornamental; sap used to make maple syrup

● **Status**
Common

variable in shape. Most maple species have green flowers, although they may be difficult to notice due to their color. The flowers are small and appear in clusters.

Hard and soft maples

Maples form two groups: hard maples, such as the Sugar maple (*Acer saccharum*); and soft maples, such as the Red maple (*Acer rubrum*) and the Silver maple (*Acer saccharinum*). The terms "hard" and "soft" refer to the strength of the tree's timber. There are 13 maple species native to the United States. Several others have been successfully introduced from abroad.

The Sugar, or Rock, maple is found throughout southeastern Canada and the northeastern United States. It may grow to 75-100 ft (23-30 m) tall and its trunk from between 3 to 4 ft (1 to 1.2 m) in diameter. The dense, hard wood of the Sugar maple is used for timber.

The Red maple grows along the east coast of Canada and the United States, from southeastern Canada down to Texas and Florida. It takes its name from the brilliant color of its leaves, which measure 2 to 6 in (5 to 15 cm) across and often have as many as five tooth-edged lobes. Red maples may reach up to 120 ft (37 m) tall and the trunk 5 ft (1.5 m) across. Their fresh buds and seeds are important foods for gray squirrels in late winter and early spring.

The Silver maple (*Acer saccharinum*) occupies much the same range as the Sugar maple but is also found a little farther south. The leaves are about 6½ in (16.5 cm) across, bright green on the upper surface, and silvery white below. They are divided into five large, toothed lobes. Silver maples prefer a damp habitat and grow extremely quickly, reaching heights of up to 120 ft (37 m) and measuring 4 ft (1.2 m) across.

Maple syrup

The sap – a watery solution that circulates through a plant's water-transport system – of both the Red and Sugar maple is boiled down to make maple syrup. The sap is harvested each year between January and April. Mature trees are tapped by drilling holes around the trunk. Plastic funnels are inserted into the holes, and the sap drips from the funnels into buckets. The sap is collected into vast storage tanks.

▼ *The maple leaf, the symbol of Canada, is also the emblem shown on the national flag of Canada.*

▼ *The Red maple (**Acer rubrum**) bears pairs of winged seeds, called samaras or keys. The seeds of each pair are joined to form a U- or V-shape.*

NATURAL HABITAT

Red maple

See also **Squirrel**

Marlin

The marlin belongs to the family of deep-sea fish known as the billfish, which also includes the sailfish and spearfish. In the billfish family there are many great sporting fish as well as food fish. They all have long bodies and a long, pointed snout, or bill. The scales on the body are either concealed or absent altogether; the tail fin is narrow, rigid, and usually forms a half-moon shape. These and other features produce a torpedo-shaped, streamlined body that offers little resistance to the water and therefore is capable of moving rapidly through the seas. In fact the billfish are among the world's fastest fish.

▼ The Black marlin is a popular game fish that puts up a strong fight when caught. This one has been caught by a fisherman, and is trying to shake off the hook and line.

Spectacular fish

The marlin is not only one of the fastest fish over long distances, it can also take great leaps above the surface of the ocean. Scientists have recorded the marlin swimming at speeds of 40-50 mph (60-80 km/h) and jumping as far as 130 ft (40 m). With the exception of the tail fin, all of the fins fold down and fit into grooves along the body when the marlin is swimming at full speed.

The marlin uses its long, spear-like bill to stun and slash its prey. It will dart through a school of slower moving fish, jerking its head from side to side as it swims. Then it will turn back (it can turn

in a very tight circle) and begin eating any fish that have been injured by the slashing spear. Records have shown that marlin also use their sharp bills to spear fish, although scientists do not know how often they use this hunting technique. They have also been known to drive their bills through wooden boats when they are swimming at top speed, often by accident.

Although fish make up the main part of the marlin's diet, it will also feed on squid and sometimes on cuttlefish. The marlin in turn is preyed on by sharks. Sharks are not able to swim as fast as the marlin, especially over short distances, but it is probable that the marlin cannot maintain its speed for very long and may fall victim to the shark when it has to slow down in order to rest.

NATURAL HABITAT

Marlin

Sporting giants

Marlin are the favorite game fish of many deep-sea anglers, and are particularly prized for their stamina during the chase. The largest species is the Black marlin (*Makaira indica*), sometimes confusingly called the White marlin because of the whitish sheen on the body of a dead specimen. It lives in the Indian and Pacific oceans, where it grows up to 14 ft (4.4 m) in length.

Two of the most popular sporting species in the warmer parts of the Atlantic Ocean are the Blue marlin (*M. nigricans*) and the White marlin (*Tetrapturus albidus*), both of which are terrific fighters. The Blue marlin can grow to a maximum weight of 1000 lb (454 kg). By comparison the White marlin is a much smaller fish, only 8 ft (2.5 m) long and weighing up to 154 lb (70 kg). It occurs off the eastern coast of North and South America, from Brazil to Nova Scotia.

A close relative of the White marlin is the Striped marlin (*T. audax*). Like the Black marlin it lives in the warm temperate and tropical waters of the Indian and Pacific oceans, from East Africa all the way to the coast of western America, and froma Japan as far south as New Zealand.

KEY FACTS

● **Name**
Blue marlin
(*Makaira nigricans*)

● **Range**
Worldwide

● **Habitat**
Tropical and warm temperate seas

● **Appearance**
10-15 ft (3-4.5 m); dark steel blue back, silvery white sides usually with lighter bars; average weight 400 lb (180 kg), maximum 700-1000 lb (317-454 kg)

● **Food**
Fish and squid

● **Breeding**
Very little is actually known about the breeding, but marlin form pairs in the spring and summer, which is probably their breeding time

● **Status**
Widespread

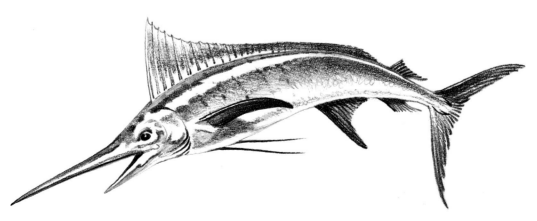

◀ *The marlin has no teeth, but it has well developed jaws. The upper jaw is drawn out into a long, spear-like bill, which is often used to stun, slash, and spear its prey — small fish and squid.*

Marmoset

Marmosets are the tiniest monkeys in the world. Along with their close relatives the tamarins, they are pretty animals, with colorful, silky hair and extravagant tufts, mustaches, or crests. There are three species of true marmoset (*Callithrix* species) and one Pygmy marmoset (*Cebuella pygmaea*). They are found in the tropical forests of northern South America.

▲ *Marmosets often look more like rodents than monkeys. They have long, sharp claws on their toes, giving them a good grip when they climb tree trunks and run along branches.*

Drinking tree sap

Marmosets are active during the day and spend most of their time foraging for food high in the treetops. This may vary from fruit and flowers to insects and small animals, although the marmosets' favorite food is the sap from trees. They get this by gnawing holes in the branches or trunks with the short, chisel-like teeth in their lower jaws, and licking up the juice that flows from the wound in the bark.

Marmosets are nimble animals and well adapted to life in the trees. Their hind legs are longer and stronger than their forelegs, giving them the power to jump from branch to branch or tree to tree. Their small size and light weight also means that, unlike most other primates, they are able to run along the smallest, thinnest branches rather than swinging through them like other monkeys.

Singing to each other

These sociable animals live in large family groups, communicating through the dark forest with pretty, musical calls that sound a little like birdsong. The groups usually consist of one adult breeding pair and their offspring at various stages of development, and they may number up to 15 animals. Each family group has a home range, which the males advertise by scent marking, gnawing at the bark on a tree branch and then covering it with urine.

If any intruders from a neighboring group enter their territory, the resident marmosets set up a chorus of loud, shrill calls to warn each other, and they attempt to chase away the unwelcome visitors, flaunting their beautiful tufts and crests as they do so. If this method does not work, the males turn their backs, lifting their tails and displaying their bright white rumps, at the same time giving off powerful pheromones (chemical signals) to frighten the intruders away.

Mother's little helpers

Female marmosets stay with the same group for life. Only one female in each family group breeds at a time. She is paired with one male, although she may occasionally mate with other males in the group aside from her partner. Some scientists believe that she may stop the other females from wanting to mate by giving out powerful chemical signals, or even by threatening them visually!

NATURAL HABITAT

Common marmoset

▲ *This strange animal is a Pygmy marmoset – the smallest monkey in the world! It grows to only 15 in (38 cm) from head to tail (the tail is more than half this length) and weighs 4 oz (120 g).*

The dominant female is a fast and successful breeder. In ideal conditions, she may give birth once every five months – usually to nonidentical twins. These baby monkeys are fairly large and heavy when they are born (usually as much as 19-25 percent of the mother's weight).

The mother finds it very difficult to carry both her offspring as well as catch food to keep herself and them alive. For this reason, the father, brothers, and sisters help out, taking turns carrying them while the others catch the food.

The baby marmosets are dependent on this help for the first two weeks of their lives, although they are able to move about and catch food for themselves at about two months old. Even when they become fully adult at two years old, they remain in their family group, helping to take care of the next offspring.

KEY FACTS

- **Name**
  Common marmoset
  (*Callithrix jacchus*)

- **Range**
  Northeastern Brazil

- **Habitat**
  Tropical forests

- **Appearance**
  A small monkey, rarely growing larger than 10 in (25 cm), with a long, ringed tail measuring up to 14 in (35 cm); long, soft, and silky hair, gray brown in color with large, contrasting ear tufts and a white blaze across the forehead; both sexes are very similar in appearance

- **Food**
  Fruit, flowers, tree gum or sap, insects, spiders, frogs, snails, lizards, small birds, birds' eggs

- **Breeding**
  2 offspring born at a time (nonidentical twins), which are relatively large and heavy at birth; at first they are carried around by other members of the group, but can move about independently at 2 months old

- **Status**
  Widespread

See also **Tamarin**

Marsupial mole

The Marsupial mole is a small, furry animal that is found only in Australia. Despite its name, it is not actually related to other moles such as the Eastern mole or the African golden mole, but, like them, it lives in the ground, digging into the sandy soil and feeding on insects and insect larvae. Indeed, it is the only Australian mammal that has adapted to this kind of burrowing and belongs to a family of its own called *Notoryctidae*.

Digging in the desert

The Marsupial mole lives in the Australian deserts. Its soft, silky, golden fur blends in with the sand, and it is well camouflaged against enemies such as dingoes. It is about the same size as an Eastern mole: it measures up to 8 in (20 cm) from head to tail and its body extremely sturdy. It is usually nocturnal (active at night) and is only very rarely seen by humans.

NATURAL HABITAT

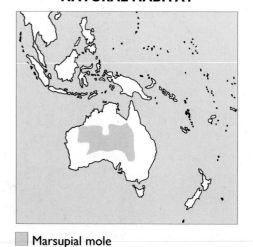

Marsupial mole

The Marsupial mole is well adapted to a burrowing way of life. It has a large, horny shield covering its snout that it uses to push forward through the sand. It also has short, powerful forelimbs with strong, triangular claws on the third and fourth toes. These claws act like scoops when the animal is digging. The bones in the mole's neck are joined to one another, making the body very rigid and strong so that it can push through the ground more easily.

However, the Marsupial mole does not spend as much time burrowing as true

▲ *This marsupial mole is burrowing into the sandy soil of the Australian desert. You can see clearly the strange triple tracks left by its two hind feet and short, stumpy tail as it shuffles along the surface.*

KEY FACTS

● **Name**
Marsupial mole
(*Notoryctes typhlops*)

● **Range**
Parts of Australia

● **Habitat**
Deserts

● **Appearance**
A small, stout body, measuring 3½-7 in (9-18 cm) with a short, stumpy tail; a large, horny shield covering the nose; triangular, scoop-like forefeet; no eyes or external ears; the females have a pouch with 2 teats; the fur is soft and silky and white, pinkish-cinnamon, or rich golden red in color

● **Food**
Insects and their larvae, particularly those of beetles, moths, and ants; some seeds

● **Breeding**
The female gives birth to a single young , which is very undeveloped at birth and carries on growing inside a pouch on its mother's abdomen where it suckles her milk

● **Status**
Common

moles and does not dig down as deep. It spends most of the time at a depth of about 3 in (8 cm), foraging for insects and their larvae – especially those of beetles, moths, and ants. A sense of smell is important for this because it cannot see, and its ears are simple openings hidden beneath a covering of fur. It may rise to the surface, where it shuffles along rapidly, leaving peculiar tracks in the sand.

"Swimming" through the soil

Unlike other moles, the Marsupial mole does not dig a large network of permanent tunnels and burrows. As it scoops out the sand with its forefeet, its hind feet throw it up and backward, giving the effect of "swimming" through the ground. And as the animal then moves on, the walls of the temporary burrow or tunnel collapse behind it.

Little is known about the Marsupial mole's breeding habits, but the female is thought to give birth to a single young in a burrow deep within the ground. In common with other marsupials, this baby is tiny and undeveloped when it is born – it has only been growing inside its mother for about a month.

As soon as it is born, the young mole makes its way to a special pouch on its mother's abdomen, where it immediately attaches itself to a teat and begins to suckle. Here it stays, slowly growing and developing until it is able to survive in the outside world without the protection of the pouch.

▼ *This is a rare closeup of a marsupial mole, showing its soft, golden fur, the huge claws on its forefeet that enable it to dig so effectively, and the large, leathery shield covering its nose.*

See also **Desert, Mole**

Meerkat

The dry scrub and grasslands around the Namib and Kalahari deserts are dotted with termite nests – piles of mud built up to protect the thousands of insects that form well-organized social groups. And these insects are in turn fed upon by another well-organized group of animals, the meerkats. They make their homes in and around the termite nests and spend hours on end standing guard, often on top of a termite mound, while other members of the group forage and feed. Some of the world's leading naturalists have done in-depth studies of the meerkat because of its fascinating family life.

Adapted to the desert

Meerkats are small mammals, looking rather like raccoons, but they actually

▼ *A female (possibly an "aunt" rather than the mother) guards three young meerkats. Other group members have their own tasks.*

belong to the mongoose family, many of which are solitary, living on their own rather than in groups. However, meerkats have found that there are great benefits to living together in social groups in their open, semidesert habitat. Besides their

NATURAL HABITAT

Meerkat

sandy coloring, meerkats have many other adaptations to life in very dry parts of Africa. They have long claws for digging burrows, which provide shade from the sun (particularly important for the newborn meerkats, who are hairless) and shelter from predators; they have keen eyesight and sharp hearing for detecting predators; and they have thin fur that does not hold in the heat.

Division of labor

Like human society, the meerkats within a particular group have different jobs to do. The group is led by an older male and he mates with the leading female. Each year, her litter of two or three young is cared for by older meerkats, the sisters of the new litter. These aunts or babysitters may have their own litters, and often nurse each other's young. Other meerkats act as teachers, showing the growing meerkats how to forage for food.

It is often the males who act as sentries, standing up on their hind legs, in trees or on top of mounds, scanning the skyline for predators – mainly birds of prey. At the slightest sign of danger, the sentry lets out an alarm call, and all the members of the group scurry off into the protection of their burrows. Other members of the group act as hunters, foraging for new sources of food.

The females usually stay with the group, and when the oldest, breeding female dies or can no longer produce a litter of her own, one of her daughters takes over. Males from the group, on the other hand, move away and live with other "adolescent" males. When they are fully adult they may

form raiding parties, trying to capture females from groups nearby in order to set up their own breeding colony. In some closely related species of mongoose, outsiders have been observed to move in to a family group, gain acceptance, and take over the tasks they do best.

▲ *Alert and on guard, this meerkat is on the lookout for predators. Its sandy brown coat merges with the baked ground behind it. Meerkats hold their forelimbs close to their body, in a very human-looking pose. Their tails are held out behind them to help them keep their balance.*

KEY FACTS

● **Name**
Meerkat or suricate (*Suricata suricatta*)

● **Habitat**
Deserts and dry grasslands

● **Range**
Southwestern Africa, including Angola, Namibia, South Africa, and Botswana

● **Appearance**
20 in (50 cm) long, including the tail; a long thin body; a long snout; sandy brown back, flecked with paler color; paler face, belly, and legs

● **Food**
Omnivorous: insects, small mammals, birds, and reptiles; birds' eggs; fruit and other plant materials

● **Breeding**
Live in complex social groups, led by a breeding male; females give birth to 2-5 young at the end of the rainy season; a gestation period of 11 weeks

● **Status**
Common in limited area

Merganser

The merganser is a streamlined bird with a long, slim bill, a fairly short neck, and a body that sits low in the water as it swims. Mergansers are members of the duck family, but unlike most of their cousins they are normally found in saltwater habitats rather than on rivers and ponds. They are superbly adapted to swimming and diving for their favorite food – fish.

There are three species found in North America. The Red-breasted merganser (*Mergus serrator*) and Hooded merganser (*Lophodytes cucullatus*) have beautiful coloring and fine crests, while the Common merganser (*Mergus merganser*) is predominantly black and white with a crest that points downward so that it cannot be seen. The Common merganser is known as the goosander or sawbill in Europe. The Red-breasted merganser is also found in Greenland and Europe.

Fishing for food

Mergansers spend their days swimming in the sea along the coastlines of the Pacific and Atlantic Oceans, searching for fish. Sometimes they are seen on freshwater lakes or ponds. They can swim rapidly because of their streamlined shape; then they suddenly dive beneath the surface, chasing minnows, killifishes, sticklebacks, or immature fish. They also eat frogs, aquatic salamanders (lizards), small crustaceans, mollusks, aquatic insects, and roots and stems of aquatic plants, according to whether they are in fresh

or salt water. They are expert divers and swim swiftly underwater in pursuit of their prey. Once they have caught it, they use their bills to grip the fish. These bills have serrated edges, so they act like teeth in cutting up larger pieces of food. These saw-like edges give them one of their common names, sawbill.

The mating game

Like many ducks, the mergansers of the northern hemisphere move north to breed, often choosing freshwater habitats rather than coastal regions. When they migrate, they fly swiftly in small flocks high in the air, their streamlined shape helping to give them the speed they need.

The male crested mergansers display their plumage at breeding time. This is

▲ *The female merganser usually builds her nest in a hole in a tree near water. The nest is lined with weeds, grasses, rootlets, and down from the female's breast.*

KEY FACTS

● Name
Red-breasted
merganser
(*Mergus serrator*)

● Range
Northern
hemisphere, including
North America,
Iceland, Europe,
eastern Asia, moving
north to breed

● Habitat
Winters along coasts
and estuaries; breeds
on rivers, lakes, and
in woodlands

● Appearance
22 in (56 cm); a
greenish-black head,
separated from the
rust breast by a
white band; black and
white feathers cover
the body; long, red
bill with slight hook;
red feet and short
legs; the female is
gray with a rust head

● Food
Fishes, crustaceans,
worms, insects,
mollusks, and plants

● Breeding
Nest usually built in a
hole lined with down
from the mother's
breast; 6-17 eggs laid
May-June, female
incubates eggs for
28-30 days

● Status
Common

also the season when the normally silent
male can be heard calling to the female.
The Common merganser has a gentle
call, but the Hooded and Red-breasted
mergansers make a rasping sound. The
females have very raucous calls and are
heard more often than the males.

The eggs are laid in a nest, often in a
tree or crevice but sometimes on the
ground. The male abandons his partner
after mating. Females often group
together to share the work of rearing their
large broods, particularly in the case of
the Red-breasted merganser. After
breeding, the males loose their display
feathers and look more like the females.

Rarer cousins

The Brazilian merganser is the only
member of the group that is found in the
southern hemisphere. According to some
scientists it is now threatened, due to

NATURAL HABITAT

☐ Red-breasted merganser

destruction of its habitat. The Scaly-sided
merganser (*Mergus squamatus*) is found in
Manchuria and Siberia in Asia. The
Auckland Island merganser from the
Auckland Islands (off the coast of New
Zealand) has been extinct since the very
early nineteenth century.

▼ *These Red-breasted mergansers in Alaska are*
wearing their winter feathers. When the spring
arrives they will develop their red breasts.

See also **Duck, Tide pool and coast**

Millipede

Millipedes are sometimes called "thousand leggers" (from *milli*, Latin for thousand). These creatures were among the first animals to live on land. They have been found in fossil rocks that are over 400 million years old.

Millipedes have changed little since that time because they were already well adapted to the habitats where they are still found. However, the living species are much smaller than some of their ancestors: in the past some of the giant species were over 6 ft (1.8 m) in length.

Today there are more than 7500 species of millipede that are found in most places where plants grow. Nearly all millipedes are vegetarians or scavengers, feeding on rotting leaves, fungi, dead animals – even tortoise droppings! They occur in large numbers in some forests where they play a major role in breaking down plant material to make soil.

Different shapes and sizes

Although most species are only an inch or less (2-25 mm) long, some tropical millipedes can grow to over 12 in (30 cm). Their bodies are segmented and covered with a hard, shell-like substance called an exoskeleton (a skeleton that is on the outside of the body).

Millipedes come in several different shapes; they can be cylindrical, flattened, or short and rounded like a sow bug or woodlouse. They have a pair of short,

NATURAL HABITAT

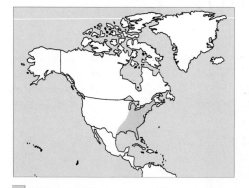

Millipede (*Narceus* species)

▲ *Some of the millipedes from tropical climates have bright colors and may grow to a large size. This Giant millipede from Venezuela may grow up to 4 in (10 cm) in length.*

▶ *Most millipedes rely on their tough exoskeleton and their ability to roll into a tight spiral to prevent predators from eating them.*

clubbed antennae on their heads and most species have between 100 and 200 eyes, although some species that live in dark cave habitats are completely blind. Millipedes breathe through tiny holes called spiracles that run the length of their bodies. There are four spiracles on each of the body segments.

In spite of being called millipedes, these creatures do not have anywhere near a thousand legs. The species with the most legs, which comes from tropical Africa, has up to 375 pairs of legs. (There are no legs on the head, tail, and reproductive segments.) Typical species such as the North American *Narceus* millipedes have between 100 and 160 legs.

Life under a rock

Millipedes usually avoid bright light and so they live under rocks, logs, and leaves, or just below the surface of the soil. They cannot survive dry conditions for long because they do not have a thick, waxy coating on their exoskeleton. If they are exposed to dry heat for too long they lose all the water from their bodies and die.

At first glance millipedes look harmless, because they do not have any sharp claws or fangs, but most species are able to put off would-be attackers by using very potent chemicals. These chemical defenses are usually used only as a last resort. If predators attack and damage the exoskeleton, they ooze a brown liquid from the holes in their sides. If the attacker then tries to eat the millipede it tastes disgusting.

Larger species such as those from Southeast Asia can squirt the chemical over a distance of 18 in (45 cm). If the chemical gets into a predator's eyes it will blind it, at least temporarily. If the predator tries to swallow the millipede it will suffer acute burns to its throat and be unable to function normally for a while.

KEY FACTS

● **Name**
Millipede (*Narceus* species, includes the Common eastern millipede)

● **Range**
Native to the eastern United States; they have been introduced to most other parts of the world

● **Habitat**
From forests to backyards, in the surface soil, or under leaves and logs

● **Appearance**
Large millipedes up to 3 in (7.5 cm); the dark-brown to black body is cylindrical; over 100 short legs; club-like antennae; 40 simple eyes

● **Food**
Herbivorous, feeding on decaying and fresh vegetable matter

● **Breeding**
Lays clutches of eggs in chambers under the soil, approximately 50 eggs laid in each batch; the female often guards the eggs against predators and regularly cleans them to keep them free of fungus

● **Status**
Widespread

Mimosa

If you touch the delicate, green, fern-like leaves of the Sensitive or Humble plant, you would immediately notice that the leaves fold up and droop. The reaction is so quick you might think that the plant had died. This amazing sensitivity to touch is an adaptation that the plant uses to avoid being eaten by predators such as insects and grazing animals.

Action and reaction

The Sensitive plant (*Mimosa pudica*) is a shrub-like, spiny-stemmed plant often found sprawling over the ground in tropical regions or forming a small bush up to about 2 ft (0.6 m) in height. Its leaves are feathery and fern-like, a delicious and tasty meal for leaf-eating insects or grazing animals. When a hungry grasshopper lands on the open, exposed leaves, however, it is in for a big surprise. In the blink of an eye, the Sensitive plant defends itself from being eaten by folding its leaves tightly against the leaf stem. What had been open foliage now looks

▲ *The open leaves of the Sensitive plant (at left) and with its leaves closed after it has been touched (at right).*

like a set of inedible twigs. If the grasshopper persists, the folded, twig-like leaves droop. This movement may also frighten off insects who lose their foothold when they land on the leaves. Furthermore, when the stalks hang down the plant can reveal its other defense mechanism — the barbs on its stem. *Mimosa pudica* does not only react this way to insects. It also exhibits similar movements during heavy rain, at night, and when there is a rapid drop in air pressure or temperature.

How it happens

The leaves of *Mimosa pudica* may move for two

NATURAL HABITAT

■ Native area of Sensitive plant

reasons. First, they have special proteins that make them contract. Second, the water pressure in certain cells at the base of the leaflet stalks may change. When the leaflets are touched these cells lose water, which makes the leaflet stalk collapse. When the touch stimulus stops – that is, when the predator has gone – the cells soak in more (reabsorb) water and the leaflet stalks return to their normal upright position in about 1 hour.

Sweet-smelling flowers

The flowers of *Mimosa pudica* are tiny and clustered together in spherical, puffy heads. They are usually a pinkish-lavender color. The flowers produce a sweet-smelling nectar, which attracts the bees that pollinate this plant.

Most species in the genus *Mimosa* are shrubs or herbaceous plants; others are woody climbing plants or small trees. Many *Mimosa* species have prickly stems, which is another adaptation these versatile plants use to avoid being eaten.

Meet the family

The Sensitive plant belongs to the group (genus) *Mimosa*, which contains about 480 other species and is part of the larger *Leguminosae* family. Many of the plants in the group *Mimosa* exhibit an interesting reaction to touch.

Other members of the *Leguminosae* family include alfalfa, green peas, and peanuts. The fruit of the Sensitive plant resembles pea pods but with prickly edges. More closely related plants in this family are the acacias, which are also found in the tropics. Acacias are best known for their relationship with the ants that live in and defend them.

◄ *The tiny pink flower head of the Sensitive plant (Mimosa pudica). In tropical regions this plant has become a widespread weed.*

See also **Acacia, Bee**

Mink

Swimming through the water or dashing through the undergrowth like a small, brown bullet, the mink is a highly efficient hunter. Its long, thin body, bursts of extreme speed, and shiny waterproof coat allow it to pursue its prey both on land and in water.

The mink – like many of its cousins, the weasels and polecats – prefers to hunt alone. It preys on a wide variety of animals including waterfowl such as ducks and teal, fish, crustaceans, muskrats, and on land rodents, birds, insects, and rabbits.

A small, savage predator

Most solitary hunters, in species as diverse as Sperm whales and cheetahs, hunt animals that are smaller than they are. But the quick, savage mink, weighing only about 2 lb (0.9 kg), can kill animals up to five times its own size. Like the small cats, mink and other weasels deliver a

▲ *This long, slender animal, with its beautiful, glossy, and dark-brown coat, is a savage predator. It is an American mink (Mustela vison), occurring naturally throughout North America, where its prey includes insects, birds, mammals, and fish.*

precise killing bite to the neck of their prey, severing the spinal cord. The attack is so swift, and the bite so firm and final, that some animals simply die of fright from being attacked by such an unshakable little predator. Once a mink has attached itself to an animal, it holds on firmly until it stops moving. This stubborn grasp allows the mink to hold onto its prey – but it can also be dangerous. If the mink attacks a large bird and does not kill it quickly, for example, it can be carried off as the bird takes to the wing! When raiding chicken farms, a mink would rather be pulled from its den by an angry farmer than abandon its freshly caught chicken.

Waterside territories

Mink spend much of their time alone, even when not hunting. They are very territorial, defending ranges that extend up to 2½ sq miles (4 km²) and contain several dens alongside the waterways (those of males are much larger than those

NATURAL HABITAT

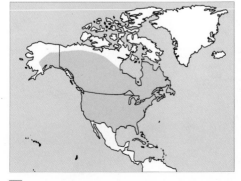

☐ American mink

of females). Both sexes mark their territories using oils from glands near the anus, which leave a strong, musky scent.

During the mating season from February to March, the males go in search of suitable females. Each mink mates with several partners. Immediately after mating the eggs are fertilized, although they do not become implanted and do not start to grow for several weeks. About a month later, a litter of four to six young are born, naked and blind. The male leaves the female to raise her offspring alone. She suckles them for eight to ten weeks and, once they reach the age of three to four months, they leave her in order to establish their own territories.

Larger cousins

There are two species of mink that are closely related to one another – the American mink *Mustela vison* and the European mink *Mustela lutreola*. Since they are up to 20 percent larger than their European cousins and have a wider range of coat color, American mink have long been bred in Europe for their fur, which is used to make fur coats. In many areas they have since escaped into the wild. Here, these feral animals (once tame and now wild) compete with the European species. Being larger, they are usually successful and force the European mink to live in poorer habitats. The two species are able to breed together. By doing this, they are rapidly becoming more and more alike, and it is often very difficult to tell to which species individuals belong.

▼ *If you look carefully, you can see a mink using this mass of roots to watch for prey. Its brown coat helps it blend in with the dead wood so that its victims do not know it is there.*

KEY FACTS

● **Name**
American mink
(Mustela vison)

● **Range**
Throughout North America; introduced into much of western Europe

● **Habitat**
Along waterways and marshes

● **Appearance**
A long, sleek animal, measuring about 18 in (45 cm) in length, with short legs, a small head and ears, and a long pointed snout; the coat is shiny brown and waterproof

● **Food**
Birds, rodents, rabbits, fish, crabs, and large insects

● **Breeding**
Males and females mate in early spring (February to March) with several partners; up to six kittens are born almost two months after mating, and the female raises them on her own; weaning occurs at two months, and the young leave their mother when only 3-4 months of age

● **Status**
Common

See also **Ferret, Weasel**

Mistletoe

Kissing beneath mistletoe at Christmastime is a time-honored tradition. Long ago, people believed that kissing beneath the mistletoe led, inevitably, to the embracing couple's marriage.

Myths and magic

Many centuries ago ancient Britons, known as the Celts, believed that the mistletoe was a sacred and magical plant. Mistletoe grows as a parasite, an organism that takes its nourishment from another organism (called the parasite's host). Celtic priests believed the mistletoe belonged to the spirit world because, unlike most other plants, it did not seem to need soil and water to grow. As a result, mistletoe was often used to ward off "evil spirits." It was thought to have healing properties. Since the plant harbors an often deadly poison in its berries, it was the leaves, rather than the fruit, that were

▲ *The poisonous European mistletoe (Viscum album), seen here growing on an apple tree branch, was once thought to be sacred.*

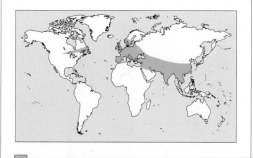

NATURAL HABITAT

▢ European mistletoe

used for medicine. So beware! The berries of mistletoe plants should never be eaten. If you suspect that anyone has eaten these extremely poisonous berries, you should contact the nearest poison center or hospital right away.

A poisonous parasite

There are 65 different kinds (species) of mistletoe in the group (genus) *Viscum*. "True" mistletoe is *Viscum album* from Europe. All mistletoes are parasites, but each species lives off a different host. Some mistletoes even live off other mistletoe species that are already living as parasites on still other hosts.

Mistletoes have separate male and female flowers, both of which are small

KEY FACTS

● **Name**
European mistletoe
(*Viscum album*)

● **Range**
Asia, Europe
(especially Britain),
and parts of Canada

● **Habitat**
Temperate forests
in the northern
hemisphere (where
its host is found)

● **Appearance**
Drooping, yellowish-
green, evergreen bush
up to 3 ft (1 m) long;
oval-shaped leaves,
leathery, up to 2 in
(5 cm) long, occurring
in pairs on forked
branches; yellow
flowers in compact
spikes; berries are
extremely toxic

● **Life cycle**
Perennial

● **Uses**
Seasonal decoration

● **Status**
Common within its
range; related species
are rarer

▶ *These parasitic American mistletoes are growing on the branches of a mesquite tree. Parasites steal water and nutrients from their host.*

and yellow. Male flowers grow on one stem, female flowers on another. In spring, the flowers are insect- or wind-pollinated. During the following winter the fruits ripen. Berry-eating birds pluck and eat the fruit, but the seeds stick to their beaks. When the birds remove the seeds by scraping their beak on a tree branch, the seeds stick to the branch.

Now the mistletoe goes to work. Special proteins, called enzymes, in the seed break down and penetrate the tree bark. A modified root forms, which grows into the living tree tissue and takes nutrients and water from the host. A thick growth of mistletoe will damage the host's branch.

Once established, the mistletoe grows very slowly. When mature, it looks like a drooping, yellowish-green bush about 2-3 ft (0.6-1 m) long, hanging from the branch of its host. The 2-in- (5-cm-) long leaves of the mistletoe are usually oval-shaped and leathery and occur in pairs on its numerous, forked branches. Mistletoe flowers form on spikes. After pollination and fertilization, the mistletoe bears berries that are toxic to both people and other animals.

Meet the family

Viscum album has many mistletoe relatives, all of which are parasitic.

The North American mistletoe (*Phoradendron serotinum*) is much rarer than its European counterpart. Another relative, dwarf mistletoe (*Arceuthobium* spp.), occurs in moderately cool (temperate) climates in the northern hemisphere and parasitizes evergreen trees called conifers.

However, most of the species related to *Viscum album* are native to the tropics and subtropics – primarily in Africa. For example, *Viscum minimum* of South Africa, parasitizes cactus-like euphorbia plants.

Does mistletoe have its uses?

Mistletoe does not have any great commercial value. Yet the use of mistletoe during Christmas celebrations is one commercial use. Mistletoe may bring us closer to a time when people were more open to the world's mystery and magic.

Mockingbird

The Northern mockingbird is famous for its rapturous singing. It has a very musical song with almost endless variations, but it also has an amazing ability to copy other sounds it hears. The Northern mockingbird is only found in the southern states and Mexico, and other mockingbird species are only found farther south; but there are several closely related species that are found in most parts of the United States. The Gray catbird, like the mockingbird, gets its name from its distinctive call. It makes a mewing sound, and sometimes attempts to copy the songs of other birds.

All year round, mockingbirds can be seen hopping through the undergrowth, using their sturdy beaks to probe for insects, seeds, and berries. Every now and then they raise their wings to disturb any insects that they have not spotted with their beady eyes.

Copycat

The mockingbird can imitate the songs of other birds so expertly that even electronic analysis cannot tell the copy from the original. Its repertoire may include the songs of as many as 36 different birds. It has also been heard to copy the sounds of other animals including frogs, dogs, and hens and even a piano and human voices.

► *The Northern mockingbird sings his remarkable song from a high perch. He stakes out the territory and keeps away any intruders. Competitors for food include robins, starlings, and other mockingbirds.*

▼ *This mockingbird, a tropical relative of the Northern mockingbird, has crept up to steal fruit from the table.*

KEY FACTS

• **Name**
Northern
mockingbird
or mockingbird
(*Mimus polyglottos*)

• **Range**
From eastern U.S.
to California

• **Habitat**
Usually lives as a
year-round resident
in trees or shrubs in
suburban or country
gardens; the edges
of open woods,
pastures, farm hedges

• **Appearance**
9-11 in (22-27 cm)
long; sexes alike;
dull gray above, paler
below, white wing
patches and white
outer tail feathers
conspicuous in flight;
a long tail

• **Food**
Grasshoppers,
beetles and other
insects; snails, lizards,
snakes, fruit

• **Breeding**
Nest built by male
and female, usually
3-10 ft above ground;
eggs laid Mar-Aug,
3-6, usually 4-5;
female incubates the
eggs for about 12
days; both parents
feed the young

• **Status**
Common

As yet there is no simple explanation for this copycat behavior, but it is probably connected with marking the bird's territory. The mockingbird sings all year round, but it is particularly tuneful when it is defending its territory in the spring or the fall. Most birds only protect their territory during the breeding season, keeping predators away, but the Northern mockingbird also fights off intruders in the fall, trying to stop other birds from eating its supply of winter food. This territorial behavior can be vicious: mockingbirds will fly at other birds and even attack cats and humans who intrude.

Nesting time

The breeding season starts in March, with mockingbirds pairing up to build a nest, usually in a small bush, or on a cactus plant. The female takes charge of the eggs, but both birds feed the young. The pair may raise several broods each year.

The Northern mockingbird has strong associations with the southern states and is the state bird of Arkansas, Florida, Mississippi, Tennessee, and Texas.

NATURAL HABITAT

Northern mockingbird

Index

> Page numbers in **boldface** type show full articles